"A first-rate book, 5 Stars" Ed

"Without doubt the best book on Leadership there

David Gillespie
Actor, Bestselling Author, Communication Consultant

"Chris does a masterful job of distilling the intricacies of leadership down to a critical truth: "There isn't good or bad leadership...You are leading or you are not." This important truth forces people to look at their approach to leadership in a very honest light. He also encourages everyone to view themselves as a potential leader because, as he reminds us, you do not have to be the best at any particular skill to excel as a leader. Most importantly, Chris reminds us that the evolution of our world has led us to a place where the keys to leadership in business as well as the military include flexibility, the freedom to maneuver, and mutual trust between leader and followers."

Lisa Petrilli
Chief Executive Officer, C-Level Strategies, Inc.
Author: The Introvert's Guide to Success in Business and Leadership

"Leadership has never been about the rank, the position you hold, the title you wear, time in grade, where you are in line, nor where you sit on the totem pole. It is always about the example you set. When you set an example for others to follow, people take notice. And you have made a difference. Chris shares with you his extensive experience from the British military to clearly emphasize the responsibility we all have to be great leaders for those around us. 'The Leadership Secret' is an excellent go-to for the person who cares about developing a style of leadership that affects everyone, in all walks of life, for all the right reasons."

Keni Thomas
Author: Get it On!: What it means to lead the way

"If you only ever read one book on Leadership, make sure it's this one."

Kevin Godlington
Entrepreneur and Philanthropist

"The Leadership Secret provides practical lessons in leadership that can be applied immediately to improve your personal performance. Chris synthesizes the lessons learned under stressful leadership situations and applies them practically to today's business environment. Every reader will extract immediate value and can use this as a reference to continually hone their leadership skill."

Martin Coyne II
Founder CEO Learning Network

The Leadership Secret

Be the Difference
That makes the Difference

Chris Whipp

First Published in 2013 by Matador

Copyright © 2013, 2015, 2022 Chris Whipp

All rights reserved.

ISBN: 9798367541007

For Paige

CONTENTS

	Introduction	Page 1
1	What is a Leader	Page 8
2	Getting to Know Your Staff	Page 16
3	Getting to Know Yourself/Your Self	Page 45
4	Discovering a Leader's Courage	Page 56
5	Learning Emotional State Control	Page 67
6	Developing Your Team	Page 94
7	Utilising Mission Trust	Page 105
8	Looking to the Future	Page 114
	Bibliography	Page 118

Introduction

"As the World's population expands and evolves, So must our approach to Leadership."

In the summer of 1996, I attended a barbecue in the garden of a countryside pub somewhere in Oxfordshire. The weather was fine and the garden was full of friends and the families of the seventy-plus guests of honour, in all more than 200 enjoying the sunshine. Children were playing on the slides and the smell of the charred burgers and sausages hung in the air. It was a celebration for a returning Troop, having recently completed a 6-month operational tour in the Balkans supporting NATO's Implementation Force. For some it was the first time they had seen their loved ones since the previous Christmas Eve and emotions were running high. Those left behind had been living with the worry of knowing those deployed were in an unforgiving and often dangerous place. The civil war had claimed literally countless lives; some estimates exceed 100,000. It was a real concern for the families and friends, since entering the area a few years earlier the British Armed Forces had already seen over 30 personnel killed, 7 during our tour including a soldier from our Regiment. Over 70 would eventually lose their lives in the zone. As a young 2nd Lieutenant and the Troop Commander, I was truly humbled by the words of the father of one of the soldiers there that day. "Thank-you for bringing my son home." He said as he shook my hand. It took me some time to realise the importance of what he said next. "It is clear to me why you are a good leader." He then went on to tell me why…

THE LEADERSHIP SECRET

***

I was the 3,750,384,624th person to be alive on the planet when I was born. Just over 50 years later the world population has exceeded 8 billion and by the year 2050 it is predicted to reach 10 billion. Never before has Leadership been so important to the world. I have been fascinated with leadership for over 30 years. In the spring of 1984 on my school report whilst distractions began to affect my overall grades my teacher had written "...and [Chris] is a good leader," I was 13 years old. I spent nearly 17 years as an officer in the British Army achieving the rank of Major in the Army Air Corps and served operationally in many theatres. Since leaving the Army I have run my own businesses and worked as an associate for many others. I have trained Doctors in 'leadership under traumatic conditions' and Managers in how to develop their team. My work has taken me from 'The City' to the frontier markets of Africa, working in corporate training for some of the wealthiest companies in the world and negotiating agricultural land deals and corporate social responsibility projects with some of the poorest people in the world. I am fortunate to have received arguably some of the best official training in the art of leadership at the Royal Military Academy Sandhurst added to that the experiences I have gained and lived through before and since have equipped me well. It has been interesting to learn what people in corporate environments think of military leadership; there are more subtleties than you might imagine. I have studied leadership, led others and experienced leaders at a variety of levels. This book is about what works and how to apply it.

A good Leader will get the best out of any team and collectively they will then perform to the best of their ability. They will create a pleasant, professional working environment conducive to success. A bad leader however, will create angst and stress, thus limiting the collective outcome. It would be wrong to suggest that bad leaders do not succeed, as history shows us that this is not the case. What is certain is whatever success a bad leader achieves they undoubtedly could have had more of it and probably been a lot more popular along the way. This book is not about dictatorship, nor is it about succeeding at all costs and 'screw anyone who gets in the way', metaphorically speaking. It is about developing leadership that instils respect for the right reasons. This is also not a book

Introduction

for those who believe that good Leaders are only good when they have made millions of pounds and drive expensive cars. This book will show that true leadership both applies to, and affects everyone in all walks of life. In the context of this book, let us assume that there is not good or bad leadership, there is either leadership or there is not. As Yoda, from Star Wars, said, you either 'do or do not'. Though a fictional character, he brings us to the first piece of good news; you cannot be a bad leader. You either are a Leader or you are not. The next piece of good news is that we all have the capability of being a Leader; it comes down to how much we care.

If we take a moment to look around, we are able to witness the creativity of human beings everywhere. It is inspiring to think that every single manmade object began as an idea in the mind of someone. From the smallest gadget to the largest building, even some of the seemingly natural landscapes are all products of the human brain. What is less obvious to some is that to make all of these things a reality, took leadership. Leaders affect our whole lives; sometimes they can be observable, like figures in the public eye. Often times too they are less obvious and behind the scenes. The countless interactions we experience every day when we travel, purchase goods, dine out, exercise and of course in our jobs are directly affected by those in a position to lead. How that interaction is played out with the 'front of house staff' is more often than not the result of the leadership of those directing those you are interacting with. As children we pick team captains for a kick around in the park long before teachers and managers decide for us. Schools have prefects, cadets have rank structures, student unions have heads and ballets have a lead dancer. Every parent, uncle and aunt is a Leader. Leaders are essential to human existence.

Throughout history, as societies have continued to evolve, the necessity for leadership styles to adapt is critical. In the past, leadership and success were measured by one's hierarchical position. Today, we must be more progressive and think not that one's position is a measure of success but of one's approach within their position; we have all had impossible bosses. Nor is it the case that the Leader is the one who is required to be the best in their field, these views are outdated. Leaders of course must have a level of competence or no one would follow them. A Leader is skillful and adaptable but being the best is not always the measure of one's ability to lead. A Leader goes beyond skill alone. You only have to look to the world of sport to notice that the best players do not necessarily make the best leaders. Arguably the best cricketer of his generation, and many other generations for that matter, Sir Ian Botham almost single-handed won countless matches for England. His fearless approach during the second half of the Ashes series of 1981 made him a household name in England; search online for 'Botham's Ashes'. However, he had begun the series as the team Captain and out of form. He had lost form ever since being given the Captaincy. The role did not suit his approach and both the team and his individual game suffered accordingly. His predecessor came out of retirement to once again lead and Sir Ian recovered his form to ensure victory. There are many other examples in the sporting world that highlight the different requirements a leader must possess over mere skill and where the highly skilled can be our greatest asset when unencumbered by official leadership.

Like a sportsman on their field of play must adapt to varying conditions, so too must the Leaders of today keep up with the important changes of growing social media. Obviously, modes of communication in the world today are developing at an incredible rate. We have been able to converse across continents with live video footage in our own homes for many years and now we can also do this from a handheld cell phone. The importance from a leadership point of view is the increase in social networking. These various sites have given people a voice. They have allowed anyone to air their views on a subject and have it seen across the world in seconds. Video footage is included too. It is said that Facebook was instrumental in the 2011 uprising in Egypt, Blackberry messaging was used in the London riots and YouTube is often the first port of call following an incident. For some journalists it has become sufficient to merely 'follow' personalities on Twitter to ensure they receive their latest quote. This communication boom comes at a price. The danger and liberation lie in the few regulations of these social media programs. As well as empowering freedom of speech and making information accessible to all, it also leaves the viewers and readers subject to fallacious claims and the unfounded opinions of anyone that cares to partake. This is especially apparent on the customer feedback sites where a high percentage of the public appear quite content to take someone's subjective opinion as an objective fact. It used to be said that if someone likes your

Introduction

product, they will tell one or two people but if they don't, they will tell seven or eight. Social networking has allowed that seven or eight to become millions. One negative comment amongst a sea of positive stands out like a warning beacon to the mind. The immediacy of these reports has also caught out the instigator on many occasions. Such is the ease in which our thoughts are uploaded and distributed, for some it is much quicker than the time taken to establish self-control and exercise a much wiser restraint.

Industry and politicians alike have seen the need to embrace this new technology. In the UK twitter users can follow politicians @tweetminster and in the US Senators are also popular tweeters. Police forces use the social network not just to promote their own work but also to identify those involved in illegal activity. Businesses everywhere are using 'virals' to promote themselves amongst an audience that previously would have been unattainable within the same budget. By understanding the power now given to anyone with access to a simple computer, Leaders of today must understand more than ever the need to get it right first time. Of course, first impressions have always counted but in reality, they were recoverable. How many times have you heard people say 'when I first met……I thought……but actually now I ……'? For that single person, the recovery may still be possible but perhaps not for the masses that one person may have already influenced. Will we still make mistakes? Of course we will but it is important that those we lead see the positive intention behind those mistakes and use them for the learning opportunity they provide.

Leadership requirements have changed and the Leaders of today and tomorrow need to develop in order to meet these requirements. Action has to speak louder than words. A positive mindset and clear direction can be an alternative to the ambiguous lists of rules and regulations that some businesses seem incapable of operating without. As someone who has learnt a lot of leadership skills from my time in the military, my transition into the business world has surprised me. The perception is often that command and control is all that is on offer from military leadership. In actual fact, as we will see, the reality of today's successful leadership in the military as in business is the development of flexibility and the freedom to manoeuvre. Allowing oneself to 'let go' sufficiently in order to develop such a working environment can be an issue for some. By the end of this book, you will see it is possible. You will trust your team and they will trust you. As your role as a Leader dictates, you will have assisted in their individual development to be positive Leaders themselves. The trust required within a team is achievable only through your actions.

Perhaps you have picked up this book because you care about your own development and want to inspire others. You may already be in or be about to undertake a position of leadership. Typically, seeking improvement is an indication of a dedicated Leader. You will quickly see that the little things are really the big things and the secret to effective leadership is not just simple but fun to apply. These are important aspects for me, fun and application. If you do not enjoy something, you are unlikely to be at your best and if you don't do it then why learn it? This is not just another clever book of observation and insight into leadership but it also serves as a usable guide to actual development. I have included examples and anecdotes of various experiences as a purposeful digression and you will take the significance of these metaphors as their relevance to you. When we watch a movie, the meaning we take from it is the meaning we most associate with at that time. I urge you to be curious and experiment where possible. We only learn to swim by getting wet. Be the difference that makes the difference. Based on past experience I am confident that if you take the time to challenge yourself and practice The Leadership Secret, you will enhance your life and the lives of those who depend on your leadership.

"There isn't good or bad Leadership,

There is Leadership or there is not.

You are Leading or you are not"

Introduction

Points to Remember - Introduction:

- Everything is affected by Leadership and everyone has the potential to be a Leader.

- As the world's population approaches 10 billion, leadership has never been more important.

- Leaders get the best out of any team.

- Social networking sites have made it possible to speak to millions in minutes; I must ensure my staff are aware of my positive intentions and develop trust.

- A positive mindset and clear direction can be an alternative to the ambiguous lists of rules and regulations.

- We can develop flexibility and freedom to manoeuvre.

1

WHAT IS A LEADER?

There are many different interpretations of what a leader is so let me be clear about what it is that makes those stand out as effective in the context of this book and those that do not. Being in a position of authority is not sufficient to make a true Leader. One who merely barks orders at their subordinates is not a Leader. History has shown that many dictators have lived relatively long and, in their own minds, successful lives, however this is often at the suffering of those over whom they dictate. As well as the fact that their lives could have been longer if it were not for the inevitable coup.

A basic requirement for an effective Leader is that they must care about leading. Leadership at any level is an honour. Taking the responsibility, however great or small, for others should not be taken lightly. It would not do, of course to be overly emotive for those under your direction but a degree of empathy with their situation will assist with your decision-making and overall influence. I have heard on numerous occasions of how a new coach or a new CEO in place has turned around the fortunes of a team. Often the first comment made about what they brought them is how much they cared. We will look more into this aspect throughout the book. You need not be overcome with emotion for the business you are in either, passion is a driving force but desperation stinks. Leading by definition implies that you are showing the way, that you are on a journey in a particular direction. It is important to remember this fact at all times. Is the team as a whole moving in the same direction? Are you developing your team? Are you developing yourself?

Can you give me examples of a good Leader? I have asked this question on numerous occasions at seminars and group discussions and I always receive similar results. Take a moment to write down the names of

What is a Leader?

five or so people that you would label as a leader.

What did you come up with? This question usually throws up heads of state from history, as one might expect and those involved in changing the world-view on human rights. They include Winston Churchill, the British Prime Minister during the Second World War, Nelson Mandela, incarcerated for many years due to the oppressive apartheid laws and eventually went on to lead his nation, South Africa. Barack Obama, the first African/American President of the United States of America. Also mentioned are top sporting personalities; Martin Johnson, England's World Cup winning rugby captain, Dan Marino, the NFL quarterback, Andrew Straus, the England cricket captain who led the team from 5th to number 1 in the world. Successful business entrepreneurs often receive high praise and special mention. Sir Richard Branson of the Virgin Group, Donald Trump and Steve Jobs are often included. All, in their own way, justifiable examples of what many would term a Leader. Added to this list often appear a few others that we do not admire, Adolf Hitler being the most common and we will stick with him as an ideal example of the point I wish to begin with. For me, Leadership and being a Leader is not just about being in charge. If I asked you whether you would like to develop your leadership style so that you too could be like Adolf, I would hope that you would answer 'no'. I am guessing that if someone described you as leading 'like Hitler did' then it would not be taken as a compliment. Perhaps there is a book on the Dictatorship Secret but I'm not sure people would want to be seen reading it.

"Leadership is Action not Position."
Donald H McGannon

One business Leader I have already mentioned, as do others more often than not when I am conducting such seminars is Richard Branson. And it is very easy to see why. Sir Richard, knighted for his contribution to UK industry and philanthropy, has managed to build a global empire continuously in the public eye whilst maintaining contact with reality. Anyone lucky enough to have travelled on his airline, Virgin Atlantic, will recognize not only the professionalism by which his staff go about their duties but also the sense of fun and cheekiness added to his information material right from the cartoon safety video through to the aeroplane shaped salt and pepper dispensers which have clearly moulded on their bases 'pinched from Virgin Atlantic'. His attitude to life is worn blatantly on his sleeve. He has been involved in some of the most exciting and daring adventures including high altitude balloon record attempts and powerboat transatlantic crossings and it is this sense of adventure that is about to take fare paying passengers into space, what more could you ask for?

I had almost completed this book when I came across this response during a BBC interview, Sir Richard gave to a question concerning his attitude to leadership and it highlights an often-misunderstood point so I just had to include it, you will see why. The interviewer is Matthew Stadlen:

MS. "Do you think you have to be, sometimes ruthless to get to where you are, to get to where you've got to?"

RB. "I think being ruthless is counter-productive. I think people like to deal with people who play fair and I think it's the stereotype of the ruthless entrepreneur pushing their way to the top. I don't think it's an accurate portrayal of how to get to the top."

And that does not mean that you allow yourself to be walked over, as he made clear with his next answer:

MS. "Are you tough though?"

RB. "Maybe. I mean if I'm taking on British Airways, I'll be tough, I'll fight my corner."

Take on BA he did and he did indeed fight his corner, in a creative and playful way, not violently. When the BA-sponsored London Eye had a technical problem that meant they couldn't erect it, Sir Richard saw an ideal opportunity. With the world's press waiting to see it going up he utilised his airship company, based just outside London, and scrambled a blimp. The end result was an airship flying over the wheel bearing the slogan 'BA Can't Get It Up!!'

For me, another great leader of our time may surprise some of you. And yet from the heart he epitomises what leadership is really all about. He first appeared on our screens back at the end of the last century and was an immediate success. Audiences were drawn in by his passion for his trade and his willingness to impart his knowledge. It was obvious to all how much he loved what he was doing and how he wanted us all to love it too. It was this infectious and driven personality that would take the

What is a Leader?

Naked Chef beyond simply having a number one bestselling cookbook. What has set Jamie Oliver apart from his peers has not simply been the engaging way he teaches us how to prepare food but his unerring drive to educate about the nutritional value of food and the damaging effect the wrong food can have on our children.

As a true Leader does, he sought to develop those around him. He took obvious delight in their success as he trained them in his own restaurant, fifteen. He then ran a campaign in the UK seeking to change decades of unhealthy school dinners served up in the canteens of the nation's education establishments. It is a recognised fact that the teenage generation of today have a potential life expectancy that could see many of them dying before their parents. What a shocking statistic. Something had to be done and Jamie set about doing it. He didn't just complain, he educated parents, children, teachers, dinner ladies and government officials on the dangers of the current diet and then provided solutions to ensure that our future generations could still enjoy their food. Let's face it, as a teenager, sweets and cream cakes seem great. It was about imparting the knowledge of moderation and healthy alternatives and of what a healthier lifestyle can allow you to do. He also took his campaign to the USA under stiff opposition and began his 'food revolution'. I would urge you to find and watch his presentation on TED.com, for which he received the annual TED Prize. It epitomises the influence you can have when you truly believe in something, when you really care. Passion is contagious. Even those who didn't necessarily believe what he was saying believed that Jamie believed it and that made it engaging and allowed them to listen to his message. It is obvious to all just how much he cares.

It is really important to remember that leaders such as Sir Richard Branson and Jamie Oliver, like all of us are human beings and therefore capable of displaying all manner of personality traits. Every single one of us is uniquely special and hidden in amongst another 8 billion at the same time. Those people that we sometimes see as infallible are just as likely to make mistakes as anyone else. A friend that you always picture as cheery is also capable of sadness. There are certain people we meet in our lives that we label as rude but is this really a fair view? Are they always rude? Even with their friends and family? It is very unlikely. The difference that makes the difference in a leader is the ability to select one's own desired resourceful emotional state, which we cover in a later chapter and their ability to interact with others that we shall also discuss.

Back to my original question, asking for examples of a leader. To develop this point, can you now take a moment to write down the names of a few people that you would call a leader but not in the public eye? Someone closer to home and personal to you.

This tends to highlight more of the attributes that really connect us to a particular leader as we explain our reasons to a group of people that do not know the person. It highlights the leadership traits that we admire. When we explain why we would label 'someone famous' as a leader we very often labour on what they achieved rather than how they achieved it. For example, someone might say that Winston Churchill was a great leader because he led his country to victory in war. When we describe someone only known to ourselves, we tend more to explain why in terms of personality traits; Mr Johnson, the teacher, was a great leader because he was always prepared to listen, to take the time to explain his requirements and we trusted him. I invite you to think again now of that list you just made of those people in your life that you would label a leader and imagine explaining to someone else just why that label counts?

The people in this group often include teachers, co-workers, friends, mothers and fathers. The explanations include words like: kind, honest, trustworthy, competent, open and strong. It is worth briefly exploring these attributes that we tend to look for in a leader as well as looking at those we do not.

So, what does a Leader have? There have been countless studies over the years to determine what it is that makes someone stand out from the crowd as a Leader. The various Internet search engines will bombard you with the results displayed however you desire: pie charts, graphs, percentages or just straight talking. Of these attributes the secret is the one that will encompass all. Before we get there let us investigate the feedback from those being led.

Honesty: This is often initially the number one quality when asked of a team. Further questioning, however, usually highlights that the attribute that is meant is **'Trust'**, as most understand that sometimes the positive intention can outweigh the action. People will forgive and overlook. Who is one of the most highly regarded US Presidents and in demand speakers? Bill Clinton, and he admitted to misleading people whilst in office.

What is a Leader?

Competence: An incompetent boss is one of the biggest destroyers of confidence and morale within the workplace. That does not mean the leader has to be the best at all of the tasks their team perform but they have to be the best they can be at their own tasks. A good understanding and recognition of the team's tasks is essential.

Communicator: Communication covers a whole realm of skills and the importance is being able to establish open lines of communication. We like to know where we fit into an organisation, to feel appreciated and valued. It is worth remembering that communication includes listening; we have two ears and one mouth. Our displayed behaviours are also a form of communicating; when you are a Leader someone is always watching. We will cover these aspects in more detail throughout the book.

Experience: Arguably experience is required before showing one's hand as a Leader. Experience can be gained in many ways and this does not necessarily mean that only the old can be effective Leaders. Everyone learns at a different rate and those able to make the most of the experience on offer will progress faster. It is often about taking advantage of the opportunities that come your way.

Charisma: We like to look up to our leaders and see them as someone dependable and exciting. We expect confidence and benefit from its contagious effect. Beware of over confidence, as arrogance is associated with a lot of other negative qualities that can lose your team.

A Sense of Humour: Yes, a sense of humour. That doesn't mean we are all looking to be led by stand-up comedians, it is merely recognition of the value of having the ability to laugh once in a while. It is often by using humour that we gain the attention of others sufficiently to pass on important information.

I do not wish to dwell on these attributes because you will find countless opinions out there and frankly it is a little obvious is it not that a lying, incompetent that cannot string a sentence together, is unable to recognise your existence let alone your ability and doesn't give a toss anyway, is unlikely to be a leader? You will find many other attributes mentioned in various studies and findings and these too are often open to a very subjective viewpoint. As an example, take integrity. Ask two people what integrity means to them and you will likely get two answers. For example, one may say something like, "It's being honest." While another may say something like "It's doing what you say you will do." Or one of

THE LEADERSHIP SECRET

the many other meanings we could attribute. We will return to this question later in the book but remember this: It says a lot about your own style as to whom you respect as a Leader. I stated that the purpose of this book was application. This is an operator's handbook and we know enough to know that if we care enough then we will get to where we want to be. For those of you who really like something to hang your hat on, then I would suggest looking at the Seven C's in chapter 7. They will serve as a good reminder.

Being a Leader is being someone who has a positive influence. A positive influence on those around them and the outcomes they seek. As we will see, Leaders are not just born they can be developed and when successful they demonstrate attributes mentioned previously as well as courage, that we will examine further, strength and wisdom, empathy, inspiration and love. Leaders are also rightfully rewarded for their efforts and these rewards will be dependent on your chosen field. There are many ways to develop your leadership skills and this book will serve as a useful guide for this. By the end though, I am certain you will have realised the true secret to being a Leader. I am not saying it is not possible to be successful in other ways and with other styles but do you want to be better? Do you want to be the best you can be? Do you want to be able to look back in years to come knowing that you did it right and by right, I mean the very best you could under the circumstances? Of course you do and if you care to, you can. In the next chapter we will look at the interaction between Leader and Team and how those being led actually know that you care.

"Serve to Lead"
Motto of the Royal Military Academy Sandhurst

What is a Leader?

Points to Remember – What is a Leader?:

- We can learn from great Leaders of the past.

- The examples you cite will give an indication to your own potential.

- It says a lot about your own style as to whom you respect as a leader.

- Leadership is determined by our actions and not the position we hold.

- Leaders have a positive influence.

- Leaders develop their teams.

2

GETTING TO KNOW YOUR STAFF

"If Motivated

you will

do it now,

If Inspired

you will

do it Forever"

Motivation is not enough. We are motivated by a variety of things. Perhaps the most obvious, especially in time of a global recession, is money. For many though, having money is just not the answer and the happiness they thought it would bring does not materialise. It is all too easy to say we want more money but it is a very empty statement if we do not know what we want more money for. What is it that we think money will give us? What will it allow us to do that we cannot do now? To say that money doesn't make you happy is a far too simplistic statement. I enjoy it when I have sufficient money to go out to dinner with friends and family or to travel. Anyone who has had an unexpected upgrade on a long-haul flight could probably recognise what an enjoyable benefit it would be to be able to afford such an experience every time. When we see a report of how a child requires money for a life-saving operation, would it not make you happy to be able to help? The thing is, we think money fixes all ills but it seldom makes a difference to the fundamental stuff. There are countless examples of lottery winners having their lives turned upside down and eventually losing all of the money they initially won and sadly along the way having lost a lot of friends. In my role as a coach, I often work with people that seemingly have it all and yet are not satisfied.

For some, money can still be a great motivator, for those who have worked out what it will give them perhaps in terms of freedom and stability it can be a worthwhile goal. For others it can be detrimental. Daniel Pink offers a, perhaps unexpected insight into the science of motivation in his book 'Drive'. Drawing on the experiences of many social science experiments he argues that offering more money as incentive can actually degrade performance in some circumstances, particularly those requiring cognition. There are some that might argue that a great deal of people directly involved in sales are totally driven by money, you may have met a few? Degradation in performance could be down to the fact that the person involved is unable to deal with the added pressure of the chance of reward. When increased value is put on something it can have a strange effect on people. If you are asked to hold a vase, I daresay that you will hold it differently or put it down quickly if told it is a multi-million dollar example from the Ming Dynasty, unless of course you have billions of dollars and then again the context can change.

People will do extraordinary things for money. On the television gameshow, The Cube, participants take part in a variety of tasks that test their reactions, agility, memory or balance (to name a few), to win an ever-increasing sum of money. As the money increases so does the pressure, as failure at the later stages means a greater loss. We will cover handling pressure in the chapter, Learning Emotional State Control, for now it is just worth acknowledging that incentives are not necessarily the answer. I would rather surprise with a reward than have it expected and we'll look at rewards in a moment.

For some it can be the fear of punishment if they do not fulfil a certain task that can be the motivation. Perhaps by the retraction of liberty. How many of us had parents that held the responsibility of tidying our room over the freedom of going out? Again though, just because there may be an unpleasant result, that is not sufficient to stop some doing it. Even the risk of death from AIDS did not stop the practice of unsafe sex. Motivation is really all about incentive, what will I get if I do such and such? It can come down to the simplicity of the stick or the carrot.

There are many motivational speakers on the various corporate circuits utilised by firms to present to their staff in an effort to motivate them to do more, to do better or in some cases to just do something. Some of the speakers are excellent and have made a highly successful and lucrative living out of their various ways of geeing up their audience. They can use a variety of methods from simply the use of language through to fire walking with varying results.

"Is Inspiration simply Self-Motivation?"

The problem for many is that the effects can be likened to that of a powerful sugar rush. The initial excitement and euphoria experienced by those fully engaged in the presentation tends to wear off over time and some can end up in a sort of motivation addiction whereby they seek the next presentation kick to keep them on their path. For these motivational junkies their dependency on an external source of direction appears to distract from the point of what the personal development industry is supposed to be all about. It is about raising awareness and passing on tools for self-application. Of course, this can be done together in presentations and seminars but there needs to be progression. On the surface this may seem like a bad idea for someone in the business of giving presentations but I think that we should demand more. I would feel dissatisfied presenting something to a group of people one month only to have to present the same thing again a month later because the effects have worn off. If they have then the effects were, well, not effective. I would rather present something one month and then later share in the success of those who took part and offer continuation training on how to progress further. To do this one has to inspire. For inspiration can be ignited from an external source but must be fueled from within. It requires an emotional connection powerful enough to keep it burning without constant attention. I would much rather offer a spark to light the fire of inspiration than offer the occasional candle of motivation.

When someone is inspired, they experience an emotional response to what inspires them. It is this internal emotion that drives people to achieve great success. When one is inspired motivation comes more from within. Clearly this still means that they can benefit from other motivational techniques and experiences but the difference is that they will continue on whatever their chosen path because of the internal emotional aspect even when external motivations are not there. When you have the ability to connect a task, a job or indeed a career to someone's emotions then they will undoubtedly give their all. Inspired people demonstrate passion and belief and this passion and belief can be infectious in terms of getting people on board and influencing their way of thinking. Think of the great orators of our time and how engaging someone can be when delivering on a subject that comes right from the heart. It is just such an engagement that you as a leader will be looking for from your staff. So, to begin with you will need to be inspired yourself. Whatever *it* is that you are looking for buying into you need to believe in *it* before you can sell that belief to others. If you don't believe in *it* then perhaps you should question why you are leading others on the same path. Maybe you just need to look at it from a different angle to gain the connection that you require. A simple technique I have found over the years when given a fairly mundane task that nevertheless still requires completion is to tie the understanding of this task to future more important events. By using it as a stepping-stone, as a necessity to greater success in the future, I feel just as committed and passionate about the outcome. It is this that keeps the flow of inspiration alive. To begin to inspire your staff, you will need to know what makes them tick. Understanding your staff is key to the shared success of the team, get to know them.

"Offer a spark to light the fire of

Inspiration

rather than the occasional candle of motivation."

You've heard the saying, right? That in business it is not what you know but who you know? There is undoubtedly some truth in that. As there is in the saying: it is not what you know or who you know, it is what you know about who you know. Getting to know your staff is imperative to the Leader.

Leaders of today must be looser in their direction of their staff in order to cope with the immediacy of the 'want an answer now' world. We will examine the 'Mission Trust' solution later in the book. A flexible, 'freedom to act' approach requires a level of trust and openness that can actually be viewed as a weakness by some hierarchical organisations. I have been involved with some very high annual turnover businesses, exceeding $1bn in some cases, and the usual answer to a new suggestion: "we'll get back to you in six to eight weeks." What is more no-one does get back to you in six weeks or eight weeks or ever and when you enquire, which is then often seen as bothering them, they respond with yet more delay because no one person can make a decision. One company even stated that they only look at new ideas once a year; they aren't doing too well at the moment. Even CEOs, put in place to make decisions often have their hands tied by bureaucracy and time delays just when a quick decision is needed most. In his book 'Loose', Martin Thomas examines this very issue extremely eloquently. He argues that the decentralisation of knowledge due to the internet has played its part in the need for less of the command-and-control approach. As I have said, becoming a looser organisation requires trust, and understanding yourself and your staff is key.

"It is not what you know

or

who you know,

it is what you know

<u>about</u>

who you know."

Just as understanding what it is that drives ourselves to want to be the best we can be, an understanding of what our staff value in life is the key. I was conducting a training day for a company's management team. During a discussion with one of the participants about the need for leaders to get to know their staff, I added an observation:

Me: "Of course, a true Leader really wants to know their staff. I like to know what they get up to in their spare time, the name of their partner and kids. I care about their life."

Manager: "That's all very well but I'm just not interested in them outside of doing their job, I don't care so long as they come to work."

Me: "Then you are not a Leader."

His reaction was one of surprise and obvious hurt that someone should cast aspersions on his own abilities not just as a leader but also actually as an effective manager. So, I went on.

Me: "How do you decide on which tool to use for a specific job?"

Manager: "Well, I just select the one that's suitable."

Me: "Based on your knowledge of what that tool can do?"

Manager: "Yes, of course."

Me: "Right, so how do you select the right person within your team for specific jobs?"

Manager: "I select who's next in line."

Me: "Because everyone's the same?"

Manager: "Yes. Well, no, they're not the same but…"

This is a common reaction. No, we are not all the same, so why do we tend to treat people the same? There are times when we generalise because we address a vast audience but even then, having the knowledge that we are different allows us to appeal to everyone using a variety of techniques. Using the above analogy, when you are a Leader, it is almost as if those you lead are your tools. Obviously, there is a lot more to people than that and I wouldn't think of people like 'things', yet they are what you have to achieve your shared desired outcomes. It is important to care about them, understand what their strengths and weaknesses are and help them develop. It is in your best interests to ensure that they are working to their best ability, for you, for themselves and for the business.

In this section we will examine how to build a better working relationship that develops trust and ensures true Leadership. In essence this is about how to ensure that your team know you care. It is up to you whether or not you do actually care but I can assure you that if you do not then, like the manager above, you will not become a true Leader. If you have never thought about it this way before then I hope it gives a real insight into the privileges that being a Leader brings and the satisfaction that comes with really making a difference. Once you do, you will find it easier to genuinely care.

Like a lot of things in life, keeping it simple makes it easier to implement. Just about everywhere I go I take my notebook or some form of note-taking device. I am not able to retain in my mind every snippet of information that I encounter. Well, I may be able to retain it but I am not able to recall it. So, to assist my memory I take notes and refer back to the notes periodically. I note down information about my staff and I read it and continually update it. I learn the name of their spouse, their kids, what they like to do in their spare time, what team they support, any particular interests, birthdays and other significant dates and just about anything I notice. I am amazed at how many managers do not do this. Utilising this information in conversation with staff has a profound effect. Think about how you feel when someone is able to specifically ask you how your children are by name, it makes it personal. If you don't have children then the effect is equally compelling when someone remembers that you had told them of a significant event coming up in your life and asks you how it went. It takes seconds and should you care to do this, the resultant communication benefit will certainly pay off.

From oxforddictionaries.com **rapport** noun. a close and harmonious relationship in which the people or groups concerned understand each other's feelings or ideas and communicate well.

Some of you may still be unconvinced about the importance of 'small talk'. A good friend of mine made his point clear about not necessarily having the time to talk for ages on the best treatment for the worming of someone's cat. Well, the time aspect is a good point, in which case it is worth remembering that you are still able to choose your moment for a discussion. If time is short then it is not the time for small talk, make the time another time. If the conversation is going on too long, you are still able to politely intervene stating that you would like to hear more at a later date. However, if I were to say that I am not interested in 'the best treatment for the worming of someone's cat', in this case, then I have missed the point. These precious couple of minutes are not about me, I am not the judge of what is important to someone else. If one of my staff has brought up a subject then it is clearly important to them and whatever I think of it, knowing that subject is extremely valuable information in getting to know that person. It will help to develop trust by showing that I care. Remember it is all relative, to them. If a director says to an actor, 'I want you to imagine that your wife has left you', in order for the actor to be authentic he needs to know whether or not his character actually liked his wife or not. The same situation could evoke sadness, relief, joy or whatever else may be relevant to the scene. I am not suggesting that if one of your staff tells you of a bereavement in the family that your first question is 'and did you like them?' That would probably appear a little insensitive.

Are you able to test yourself right now? Write down as much information as you can about your staff. How much do you really know about them? How can you use this information to begin a conversation without immediately talking about work? Perhaps you are still wondering why bother? It is very simple; by talking about a subject that is dear to someone's heart you will gain their interest and they are more likely to become engaged in conversation with you. This is all part of developing mutual trust and it really is this easy. A Leader has to develop people skills, what some term 'the common touch'.

During the 'Foot and Mouth' crisis that swept the UK in the year 2001, I was on an exchange tour to the Royal Navy flying Sea King helicopters with the Commando Helicopter Force. After planning a fairly routine training flight, we received an unexpected task. My aircraft commander and our aircrewman joined me in the operations room for some short notice planning. The then Prime Minister, Tony Blair, had been touring a number of affected farms in Wales and having extended his discussions with the farmers was now running late for an important meeting in London. To avoid cutting short the visit we were tasked with picking him up from the nearest suitable open space and transporting his entourage to Cardiff to catch a connecting flight to London. The Heddlu de Cymru, the South Wales Police, had kindly secured a field and clearly marked the makeshift landing site, which we obligingly touched down into. Inevitably the pick-up time came and went and we adjusted any bookings accordingly. Sometime later a member of the protection team informed us of the Prime Minister's impending arrival and so we got started and ready for take-off. With all that was going on in the life of Tony Blair at that time, as soon as he boarded the aircraft, he asked for a headset in order to speak with us. He apologised for any delay and disruption to our day and thanked us for helping. After exchanging small talk for a few moments, he took his seat and received his next brief whilst we took to the air. The impression he left with us all that day, despite any of our political persuasion, was profound. Despite running the country and dealing with all that that entails, he cared enough to get to know those who work for him, however indirectly, and he cared enough to show he cared. A good insight as to how he got to be where he was, from someone who actually claimed, in his book A Journey, my Political Life, to have zero Emotional Intelligence. We will cover more on Emotional Intelligence later in the book.

I have heard people say,

"I see some of my staff so infrequently that I don't have time for 'small talk', we need to talk work."

Well, good news!

When you are a Leader,

'small talk' is work.

Remember, learning this personal information and utilising it must be done with sincerity. If not, then you will just appear creepy and be unable to assert any influence. Influence is an important part of Leadership, right? Imparting your ideas and for others to act on those ideas for a specific outcome. We are talking about a positive influence, beneficial to you, them and the business; no bad leadership here! In order to influence others, we must gain rapport. It is essential to all effective communication. When people are in rapport, they develop a sense of mutual understanding and trust. The good news is that you already know about rapport because a lot of it is done at the unconscious level based on human instinct. The chances are the people, whom you choose to spend most of your time with dress, sound and behave similar to yourself. Bringing this knowledge of the subject into your conscious awareness will allow those around you the opportunity to hear what you have to say. When someone does not appear to be listening to you, it is probably because you have lost rapport.

We are free to observe natural occurrences of rapport in all aspects of everyday life. Just notice the interactive behaviour of people who get on well together. When you are chatting with your friends it is unlikely that one of you is lounging in a chair whilst the others are standing up straight as if about to meet the Queen? (Rest in peace Your Majesty) And yet some managers only ever interact in this manner of opposite posture. Have you noticed how when out with someone you like how often you will raise your glasses at the same time? Next time you are in a restaurant or café have a look at the different tables and notice those who look like they are engaged in conversation and those not, then notice the difference in their posture. Groups will tend to stand or sit in a similar fashion once in rapport. Even speech will be of a similar tempo, tone and inflection.

"If you want to be heard, listen."

I realise some of you may be thinking this body language stuff is nonsense and you are right, if misinterpreted, then it is. As an example, 'I'm not being defensive, my arms are folded because I'm cold.' The important aspects for us to take away are twofold: First, avoid a complete mismatch in body position. If you are sitting down, can they? If you are standing, are you relaxed, could it be interpreted that you are talking down to someone? Remember it is not what you mean that is important but the meaning associated by the receiver. Those of you concerned about losing respect, don't be. If you are sitting chatting to your boss over a coffee, have you lost respect for them? Second, we are not the judges of how someone feels purely by their posture. It is interesting to notice changes in body language as they offer an opportunity to enquire as to a meaning. The point being there has been a change. The only way you will notice a change is if you are aware of the norm. So be aware and be curious as to the reason for any changes.

Gaining rapport is also about how we converse. It is a great advantage to begin a conversation in agreement about a subject that you know they know too. Start with something unlikely to be contested; it could be why we seem to have developed a fascination with talking about the weather. We feel comfortable when someone points out the fact that it is raining or sunny and of course we agree because it is and there you have it, a start to a conversation. Knowing the person, as you will because they are your staff and you have taken the time to get to know them, you can begin with a subject that appeals to them. "I see your team won again at the weekend", if they did.

Combining the physiological aspects with the verbal serves to deepen the rapport. Should someone use gestures when conversing, as many of us do, then matching those gestures in a similar way will be as unconsciously welcomed as would using the same sensory-based language. 'What is sensory-based language?' I hear you cry. It relates to how we express ourselves. Some of us use words with the sense of sight predicates; you see what I mean, how does it look, that is a beautiful example. Others use auditory; I hear what you are saying, I like the sound of that, that rings a bell. And some are more kinaesthetic (feelings/sensations); this feels right, that really touched me, I am warming to the idea. Generally, we can all use a combination of different sensory-based language but it is likely that we use one more than any other, our dominant sense, also termed our 'primary representational system'. It is by bringing this knowledge into our conscious awareness that we are able to utilise the additional information on offer. The VAK (Visual, Auditory & Kinaesthetic) can also dominate how we prefer to learn. Examples could be V-reading, A-listening and K-taking part. When giving a presentation to a large audience it is advisable to utilise language that covers all senses to appeal to all.

To make best use of this information we need to develop our 'calibration skills', spotting changes in other people. The changes we are looking for are unconscious responses to a given situation. Calibration, in this context, is noticing these unconscious signals that we all display, the signals that give away the fact that something has affected us. The most obvious of these signals is a blushing of the cheeks; have you ever gone red with embarrassment or know someone who does? Our breathing pattern is almost always the best indicator of a change in emotional state, have you noticed people catch their breath when in shock?

To improve your own calibration skills and begin to notice a shift in emotional state within someone, practice watching the television with the sound off. Notice the minute muscle movements, the shifts in posture and colour changes. The lower lip often gives away a shift in state, as it is not a part of the body usually under direct conscious control. Have you ever heard someone suddenly speak in a higher pitch when defending themselves? There is an episode in the sitcom 'Friends', 'The one where Ross is fine', when Ross sees his ex, Rachel, kissing his friend, Joey. In trying to convince them and himself that he is fine about it, his voice gets higher and higher as he repeats "I'm fine. I'm fine" It's a great comedic exaggeration of what we do. These are all indicators that 'something is up' and not necessarily something bad. Remember you are not in an episode of 'Lie to Me', a Series based around an agency that use increased sensory acuity primarily with regards body language to gather the truth. Nor are you trying to be Derren Brown, the excellent illusionist and entertainer who uses a number of techniques, some covered in this book, to influence and detect emotional state shifts in his subjects during his entertainment shows. The intention is not to make a judgement about what the signal means it is to notice the signal. Noticing the signal is sufficient to allow you to then enquire as to whether there has been a misunderstanding or not.

I have no doubt that my ability to talk to people from all walks of life has been a major positive in my leadership success. As a Leader I cared enough to find out what my team cared about. During my career as an officer in the British Army on several occasions the fact that I was interested in football and indeed a lifelong Chelsea fan was the subject of some derision amongst the, how shall I put it? - More archetypal army officer with a different educational background to mine. Indeed, for some the very notion that an army officer could support a football team let alone play football would cause a severe contortion to the facial expression. As an accomplished rugby player my initial retort would be based around the

THE LEADERSHIP SECRET

fact that I'm lucky enough to be able to do both and of course the majority of them couldn't do either.

My interest in the national game I feel has certainly contributed to the ability that I have in building rapport with those entering the armed forces without a commission. You can be sure that whatever the weekend's activities on the football pitch, or off it where some players are concerned, it will be the source of constant discussion in the crew rooms, the NAAFI and bars for the week ahead. When the subject of football would be raised in the officers' mess during my later years by the junior officers, they would often jump on the bandwagon, labelling the sport as 'Kev Ball' in an effort to gain a cheap laugh and peer acceptance. I would make a point of advising them to not dismiss the subject that almost without exception every one of their soldiers would take an interest in and that they would be better served taking an interest in the game that would give them an immediate icebreaker to any conversation. 'Pick a team', I would advise, 'follow it for a few weeks just to check the results, you'll be amazed at how just a few minutes reading the back pages of the newspapers can make such a difference to how soldiers respond to your word.' This of course equates to any interest or hobby. It wouldn't matter what it was and it also would not mean that it had to become my hobby or interest but if I had a member of staff that was passionate about something then it makes total sense for me to take an interest in that something to enable me to understand that person just a little more. In one of my roles, one of my team was a parachute instructor and to get to know him better I asked him to teach me. It was a great insight into his world and following his expert instruction I found myself floating down to Salisbury Plain strapped to a piece of silk. I am not saying you need to jump out of a plane to get to know your staff, but would you?

Incidentally, at the beginning of the 20th century the British military historian, Sir John Fortescue, wrote this passage in his multi-volume work, A History of the British Army:

'Sixty years ago, if not longer, officers and men were playing in the same regimental team at cricket, but football was confined to schools and universities. Since then football has grown into a national pastime, in which the Army eagerly takes part; and the officers, not content with working with their men, have steadily played with them. In other armies such an association of all ranks on a common footing might be regarded

as dangerous to discipline. In the British Army an officer who has led his men to victory in a football match will be the more devotedly followed by them in a sterner field.'

Sir John Fortescue, A History of the British Army

An interesting insight still relevant over 100 years later, and also very simple to understand why it would be so effective.

The Commanding Officer of a Regiment hardly ever gets the chance to meet his soldiers individually, there being hundreds in a Regiment and the Commanding Officer being in post for just 2 years. As a 2nd Lieutenant, the lowest ranking commissioned officer, I witnessed my Commanding Officer on several occasions meeting his soldiers. He would shake their hand as he introduced himself, stating his position, before asking about them. Spending a couple of minutes finding out a few snippets of information of a young life in his charge. It was always a really powerful experience for the soldier and a good example to me. He was the same boss who had requested that I delay my pilots' course to enable me to deploy on an operational tour with my troop, recognising the potential negative effect that a change in command could have at such an important time. He also, more than a year after I had left his unit took the trouble to find out where I was and sent me a congratulatory message on receiving the coveted Army Pilot Wings. Clearly someone who cared, clearly a Leader.

As we have seen, rapport is about holding the willing attention of others. As it can be verbal or non-verbal it works with small children and even animals, never work with them! Being able to gain rapport with children and establish a willingness in them to listen is surely every parent's dream, is it not? Generally, you will naturally be in rapport with your own children but an increased awareness will allow you to notice when they break it and give you the necessary skills to get it back. I don't know how you feel but for me, being a parent is the most important Leadership role we will ever have?

I conducted some training for a group of Junior Doctors, Registrars and Consultants in my local NHS trust hospital. The group all worked in the Accident and Emergency department and I was there to assist with their leadership development specifically within the pressure environment of life and death situations. The training was under the banner 'Leadership and Trauma', with the emphasis on the potential psychological aspects of trauma rather than the pathological. What was interesting, and a little concerning to me, was that doctors receive no official leadership training throughout their medical studies. The reason it was concerning was because each one of them and every other doctor on an A&E ward finds themselves in charge of the team whose actions are responsible for saving lives. During my research leading up to the training I discovered a paper written in 2009 in the Scandinavian Journal of Trauma, Resuscitation and Emergency Medicine: 'Leadership is the essential non-technical Skill in the trauma team - results of a qualitative study'. The study suggested that 1 in 13 deaths, in the country involved, caused by trauma were potentially preventable. This 'potentially preventable' situation included a breakdown in the leadership dynamic. In other words, the necessary resources in terms of equipment, personnel and skills were on hand to save life but the overall leadership of those moving parts meant that required life-saving actions were not taken. When I discuss this finding with A&E staff, I am shocked to find that a great number of them are not surprised. The courage required by doctors day in, day out in an emergency room is obvious, what is not so obvious is the effect their actions have on the team around them and the repercussions thereof.

Following a question regarding how they prepare for a major trauma incident knowing that casualties are on the way, one doctor stated that he liked to make a little joke and keep things light-hearted to keep himself calm. "Great, if that works for you that's fine, and how does your team respond to that?" I asked. His face reddened as he answered, "I hadn't even thought to find out." The truth is some of his team may have welcomed that approach and some may have hated it. People react differently to any given situation and as Leaders we need to be aware of this and act on it. In the medical profession as with other skill-based professions, competency is a highly regarded attribute that staff look for in a Leader but any question of attitude will likely diminish trust and could lead to vital time delays. Only by getting to know those you lead, or calibrating their response, will you be able to decide what works and what does not and assess how the team is working together.

Getting to Know Your Staff

> *"If your actions inspire others to*
> *dream more, learn more, do more*
> *and become more,*
> *you are a Leader."*

John Quincy Adams

Some might argue that a doctor fully focused on the patient could not possibly be aware of their team around at the same time. The doctor who understands the potential difficulties for their staff whilst under such conditions will ensure they are clear and commanding in their actions and verbal instructions. They will also have prepared beforehand and will invite feedback after an event. Even if you have never met them before how would it help if you as a member of the staff knowing that casualties were seconds from the door and the doctor simply stated; 'Hello everyone, I am Doctor Smith, we are all aware of the casualties approaching following the incident earlier. I have every confidence in your abilities, let us remain professional throughout, be clear in our instructions and responses, work as a team and help each other to help the patients'. Or something along those lines, anything that acknowledges the role of the team. By saying nothing, you are still communicating but the meaning of your communication is left to the minds of others. We cannot 'not' communicate. Not talking is not 'not communicating'.

Not talking is not 'not communicating'

What is communication? If someone is told that they are a bad communicator, just what does that mean? Does it mean that they cannot speak clearly, that their emails do not make sense, that their text messages are incomprehensible, that no one understands their hand signals or that their marketing strategy is way off the mark? The word communication without specification is merely a generalisation. So how do we improve all aspects of our communication? It is really important to understand that it is not what we say but what is heard that is key. Have you ever received a message that had an emotional effect on you that totally contradicted the intention of the sender? This mind reading effect can be very damaging to relationships in the workplace as well as in our private lives.

> *"It is not what you say that is important, but what is heard."*

I remember once receiving an email from my boss, he was clearly unhappy with my work and he wished to discuss this with me at the earliest opportunity. Unfortunately, the earliest opportunity was several days later and so for those several days, as this was before I knew what I now know about emotional state control, I went through a series of emotions from anger to anxiety and I became very defensive. I built a whole scenario in my head, which I then began to live-out and by the time I eventually got to see my boss I was totally ready to stand up for myself and give him what for. Very luckily for me he was able to speak first and after handing me my coffee it turned out that he was actually delighted with what I was doing and wanted my help in how to get others to do the same, how wrong could I be? After our meeting I shared with him what I had been going through for the last few days and reading his email again he could see how I might have interpreted it in the negative sense and I could now see how positive it was actually meant. A valid lesson to us both; language is subjective. During my final tour in the army, I headed a specialised training team at the School of Army Aviation. My department included a civilian office assistant responsible for various administrative tasks. It became apparent early on that for those in green having served in various combat zones throughout the world the word 'URGENT' when left in messages should be reserved for events significantly more important than the ordering of items for the stationery store, it is all relative!

How often have we made a judgment about what someone is thinking based only on the fact that they are not speaking? As Leaders we benefit from this awareness, the knowledge that our inactions as well as our actions have an effect on those around us. It highlights the issues we face with communication. If we are not clear in imparting our thoughts, others will second guess and as with most mind reading, it will be wrong. It is better to be clear and intercept any second-guessing. Imagine a ground handler on the apron of an airport. We have all seen them with their distinctive coloured paddles or light wands. Unable to speak with the pilot but still very clear in their actions of where they wish the aircraft to go. There is even a signal for 'do nothing', why? Well, without this clear signal the communication is open to interpretation from the aircrew; are they paying attention? Perhaps we have the wrong marshaller, they don't seem to care. The fact that ground handlers wear a specific uniform, as with all uniforms, is in itself another form of communication; a single sense (visual) identifier.

"Calm down, chef!"

Have you ever watched the chef, Gordon Ramsay at work in the kitchen? On any one of his television shows you will witness at some point, Gordon losing the plot. He will shout and scream at those working in his kitchen or the waiters in the restaurant in an effort to get them to do better. His staff are often reduced to tears and certainly are unable to concentrate on the slightest direction before gaining composure. His toddler-like tantrums I have no doubt are somewhat staged for the cameras but I am certain he would get a much better response from his staff if he chose a different way to communicate. He isn't the only chef on television with this attitude, Marco Pierre White is equally dramatic on his 'Hell's Kitchen' show. I have seen people less fussed over a mortar attack than his response to overcooked vegetables. If you are one who slams the table, throws objects across the room and screams at your staff you may wish to assess how effective that is and how it looks to an observer? By contrast watching how Raymond Blanc interacts with his staff on one of his shows, such as The Hungry Frenchman, is encouraging, informative and inspiring. It shows that a kitchen does not have to be so dramatic. I know whose food I would prefer to eat.

I once found myself on the border of Sierra Leone and Liberia. The locals were showing me the transport routes across the nation-dividing Mano River. The dusty road led to a large bridge traversing the fast-running water and leaving our vehicle at the police check point, with their blessing we walked the last hundred metres for a closer look. It was hot and humid outside of the air-conditioned 4x4 but welcome relief to the bone-shaking journey of the previous two days. Set back from the road, down a steep slope sat a flat concrete building. It had probably been painted white at some point but the constant dirt and winds from the

THE LEADERSHIP SECRET

Atlantic had long disguised any workmanship from the painters. As we stretched our limbs and chatted to the police my fair skin encouraged interest from the building's occupants. The men began shouting instructions to our party and replies were offered from the police as well as my escorts. I couldn't fully understand but the gist was clear: the immigration officers down the slope had 'ordered' our party to present ourselves to them. Being on a short time schedule, the request had been that we move on seeing that we had explained ourselves to the police and had no need to cross the border. This was rejected and the police were apparently belittled in the exchange, which had subsequently got them rattled. Seeing their position undermined, the police now joined in the shouting match, by this time on the road as the officers had crested the slope. Having not brought any identification with them to the shouting match, the immigration staff had to retreat to their offices in order to continue. By now the incredibly vocal and agitated group had grown and the officers clearly felt their position to be almost ridiculed. With everyone around me having clearly lost their temper, except one of the policemen who appeared only just awake, I dismissed my desire to point out the obvious commonsense approach and instead opted to remain calm and just listen. As my friend showed my passport to the most aggressive officer, it was snatched from his hand and he marched forcefully off to his ground. His next demand was to see 'the white' in his office. The comment further enraged the group although I am sure was meant purely to avoid ambiguity, and so I followed not wishing to be separated from my passport. We thankfully passed by the door that read 'male examination room' and once in his office I listened intently as he spouted all sorts of reasons for detaining me and offered some ridiculous laws and fictitious commandments that I had apparently broken. When he finished his monologue, I thanked him for being so thorough and recognised him for doing his job. I assured him that as I had been in Parliament House earlier that week and clearly no one else was aware of this information I would take my passport to the High Commission at the next opportunity to seek assistance. Reaching for my passport I thanked him again and asked if I was free to go now. 'Your friends have done you no favours,' he said handing me the passport, the argument outside could still be heard raging. 'I am letting you go because you have been so calm.' Well, I was pretty angry inside but I certainly chose to appear calm.

Getting to Know Your Staff

It is increasingly common for many of us to have interactions with our staff or customers over the telephone. Just because we cannot be seen it does not mean that the other person is unable to determine our level of commitment to the conversation. We have all been on the phone to someone who appears so distracted that it is impossible to hold a meaningful discussion. When conversing on the telephone we would do well to imagine how we could be interpreted from the other end. Am I fully engaged in the conversation? Have I been clear in my direction and avoided ambiguity? Can I confirm that I have been understood? Am I listening? When talking on the phone it can be useful to imagine that they can see you. Would you be playing that game on the computer if they were in the room with you? Whatever the circumstance it is important to remember that when on the telephone a large amount of our personality is missing. Without the ability to see our facial expressions and animated gestures, which we still do while on the phone, the recipient only has our speech to determine the meaning. Let us not leave it up to their imagination to fill in any blanks and make our voice communication as clear as we would be face to face.

I have often been in a situation where I have had to communicate over a radio. In such a situation you only have your voice in that moment to affect the outcome you desire. Practice, preparation and clear operating procedures are key to success. I recall one such mission when I was responding to an extremely agitated voice over the radio. He had every right to be agitated as he and his unit were coming under fire and he was desperate for our help in extracting from the situation. His North American accent was distorted due to the sounds of the incoming rounds he was experiencing as well as the returning fire from his position. I strained to understand him amidst the mêlée below. Although my heart wanted to race with the excitement of the situation, I needed to remain calm, slow, deliberate and positive with my transmissions (and by positive I do not mean pretending everything is okay). In between our conversation, I was holding 3 other discussions on the further radios fitted to my office, an Apache Attack Helicopter, and a fourth on the intercom with my rear seat pilot. Each different conversation would take on its own style. Conversing with my rear seat was quick and contained a lot of familiar slang. It would also involve an element of 'small talk' and humour during any lulls in the activity that would serve to ground our situation, not literally! Any discussion with our colleagues in other Apaches would be direct and affirmative, including many abbreviations and low-level code words. The information had to be accurate and clearly understood as we were firing live rounds to within metres of our own troops. Using these varying styles, I was able to emphasise the importance of each sentence, getting my point across in the quickest possible time. I was able to direct the fire support necessary for the unit to escape to a safe area, well a safer area!

Be positive. The field of Positive Psychology is relatively new. Incredibly it has only really been in the last 25 years or so that studies have been conducted focusing on the results a positive outlook can have on life and business. By focusing on finding out how things go right for some and not others, positive psychologists, such as Martin Seligman, have been studying those who succeed. Although for some, success can bring happiness it is becoming more apparent that happiness brings success. I actually think the words 'happy' and 'happiness' are perhaps a little unhelpful as they can be misleading. If someone is laughing, are they happy or did they just find something funny? Does a smile represent happiness or contentment? Being happy can conjure up thoughts of skipping and dancing and almost a resignation that one has reached their finality. It comes across as too simplistic for what I mean in terms of focus and development. For me there is more to the positive mindset and sense of wellbeing I am alluding to, which encompasses drive, determination, engagement, meaning and anything else that suits a specific time of inspiration. It is about the internal relativity of the moment and we will cover more in the chapter, 'Learning Emotional State Control'. We are continually changing; what made me happy yesterday may not today and yet I can remain in a positive mindset, focused on achievement. It may be that for you the term happy is enough and for the rest of us it could be just a reminder to be positive. I will continue to use both terms for you to make up your own mind.

In July 2011 the golfer, Darren Clarke, won The Open at Royal St George's Golf Club in the South East of England. Viewers would have seen Darren arrive every morning with a smile on his face and heard him comment on how relaxed he was feeling. Three shots off the lead after day one by the end of the second round he was in the lead, as he was on the fourth day to win his first major title at the age of 42. The BBC presenter,

Hazel Irvine, commented during the tournament, 'no wonder he's smiling, he's leading the Open,' or words to that affect. The point is, he had been smiling from the moment he had arrived. Talking of the relaxed atmosphere created by the set up his manager, Andrew 'Chubby' Chandler, creates for his players, he spoke of how much he is enjoying his golf and how happy he is with life. Chubby's other charges had also won the previous two majors and the 2010 Open.

Of course it isn't easy for some of us to just be happy or be positive. One of the worst things to hear when you're not feeling at your best: 'Cheer up, it might never happen.' Clearly it already has, or has it? Most of the things we worry about never actually happen. Recent discoveries are dispelling the myth that we are pre-programmed to a certain level of happiness and that we have a set limit for life. It is possible to improve one's level of happiness. All very well, you may be thinking but what has this got to do with Leadership? Well, countless studies are finding that we are at our most productive when we are happy, when we are in a positive mindset. The chemical reactions in our mind initiated by positivity also put us in an optimum state for learning and awareness. This should not really come as a surprise to us; it is not often that a sad and low team are renowned for their success. The challenge for Leaders is how to make and keep your staff happy? We have already discussed getting to know your staff and how to communicate effectively. It is also important to encourage your team. Some people appear to find it very difficult to say 'well done' or 'thank you' when it is deserved.

"It's the little things that are the big things."

We are often very quick to point out where something has gone wrong and a lot slower to notice where something is going right. Have you ever worked in a department that is only noticed when it does something wrong? When it is working well with everyone doing what they should be doing achieving the results expected no one even recognizes your existence. This is often the domain of logistics. When items are delivered on time, they are often just taken for granted but when they don't turn up someone comes looking for those responsible. A Leader doesn't take things for granted; they know what it takes for a department to make it look like it runs like clockwork. A Leader notices what others do not and then makes it their job to make sure all are recognised and know about it. Speaking with a friend of mine the other day she told me that she couldn't remember the last time her employers thanked her for doing a good job. Now I hasten to add that I know for a fact that she does do a good job so it wasn't that reason that no one had thanked her. The truth is for many people saying thank you to someone for doing their job that they are paid for seems unnecessary but it is absolutely necessary as a Leader to show someone that you recognise their effort and achievements. You may well receive the reply 'I was just doing my job' which is great, you are also doing yours by letting them know you appreciate theirs.

Develop loyalty share success. It amazes me how often I see business leaders not prepared to share success with those that helped create it. Apart from the obvious indication of greed and a lack of awareness, they are also missing a valuable tool in the development of loyalty. We will discuss further in the chapter, 'Utilising Mission Trust' how people very often want to feel like they belong to an organisation and that their efforts are recognised.

When times are good and profits high if you are able to share those profits, at least a fraction of them, with those that help you make them, will go a long way to build a sense of belonging and develop real loyalty amongst your team. It isn't always possible to simply give all members of staff more money out of the profits although clearly a monetary bonus would be highly desirable to some. When simply giving extra money is not an option it is up to the Leader to determine what is possible and of course knowing your team will help you make a popular decision. The following are a few bonus ideas I've either used or heard about:

- More money. (We've covered this one.)
- A team night/day out. (If it is a team bonus.)
- A late start or early finish.
- A parking space. (A really good employee of the month incentive where parking is at a premium. I've used this before with a parking space allocated near the main entrance. A word of warning if your staff includes surf dudes with highly decorative 'passion wagons' then you may need to add a caveat although I kind of liked the originality.)
- Meal for two. (This can work as an excellent bonus that recognizes the support given by a spouse. I witnessed a managing director

announce this gift to his senior management team emphasising his request that each and every one of them pass on his thanks to their individual partners for the support they give throughout the year. The team were incredibly touched by this gesture especially one who had only joined the company within the last month, imagine what that did to back up her recent decision. Such a simple and reasonably cheap bonus that carries a powerful and valuable message.)

- Gym membership. (Healthy staff means less sick days, bar injuries.)
- Extra time off. (It doesn't have to be days, what about an afternoon off for Christmas shopping?)
- Free refreshments.
- Opportunities for personal development.
- Career courses.
- Tickets to specific events. (This is where your knowledge of their favourite football team or interest in music or the theatre will pay dividends. What about a family ticket to the pantomime?)
- An iTunes voucher (I think they start at 99 pence).

Can you think of any of the above that you could use or indeed any others more relevant to your own business and staff? Of course, you could always ask your staff.

The positive effects this can have on staff cannot be underestimated. Remember, as discussed earlier, these are not meant to be used as 'carrot incentives' prior to the work. When someone believes their efforts will not only be recognised but rewarded this is a major incentive in itself. It will also give employees a sense that what happens to the business really matters to them and this will encourage them to learn more about the business as a whole. The whole experience will go a long way to developing loyalty amongst your staff and trust. When people know they will be rewarded during the good times they are more likely to help you out of the bad times. Less staff turnover means greater experience, less initial training and hopefully a greater sense of belonging all of which will benefit the customer.

*"A little less conversation,
a little more action, please."*
Elvis Presley

THE LEADERSHIP SECRET

Meetings, meetings and more meetings! Can you estimate how much of your life has been spent in meetings? I dread to think. I do know that a great deal of time that I used to spend in meetings was spent trying to get out of the next one. As Leaders, it is vitally important to communicate with our staff, as it is with our peers and our superiors, and holding a meeting can be an ideal platform for such an experience. How often is it used correctly as a valuable use of time? It is up to the Leader to lead the meeting. Have you ever left a meeting with more questions than answers? Felt like you have gone backwards rather than forwards? With the only result being that there would be another meeting and even the date of that had not been agreed on? Let us start with regular scheduled meetings. The 'every Monday at noon' type affairs that some managers seem to believe that they have to have. With the misconception that having a meeting is progress; it is not. Often the 'regular scheduled meeting' can get in the way of progress because it blocks out a period of potential activity.

What goes on in a meeting can be progress but a meeting alone is definitely not progress. The problem with regular meetings can be that often it is seen as the only moment to bring up one's issues. I have seen people sit on an issue for 6 days, until the next meeting, rather than seek a solution immediately. Inevitably the issue is therefore greater. What about when a meeting is actually a conference call? I have taken part in some toe-curling oversubscribed calls where, with the wonders of modern technology, those involved spanned 3 continents. Through good intentions each individual member wished to say hello with every other individual before unloading a weeks worth of issues pertinent to a minority of the group. Add to this the inevitable dropping offline and then the over polite apologies after reconnection, these brain numbing calls would end up having to be cut short in terms of agenda if not of time.

The key to a successful meeting is in the 'framing', how you set it up in terms of intention. What is the point of the meeting? Once this is clear and agreed on, then it is important to remain on topic to ensure progress. If at any time the discussion is wandering then it is important to go back to the agreed frame and reiterate the intentions. Is it possible to share thoughts prior to the meeting, in advance, rather than sitting on information? Unless it is your birthday, you probably don't want a surprise! By giving your staff time to consider the agenda and your thoughts prior to a meeting, on their own, you are more likely to receive solutions rather than initial reactions.

"We are what we repeatedly do, excellence, then, is not an act, but a habit."

Aristotle

There are many who believe that the environment we are brought up in is solely responsible for who we will be. I disagree. The character of some is sufficient to be their best whatever the circumstances they find themselves in. It is far too often that excuses are found to make up for a lack of drive. I have done it myself: My school academic results are not that good because the school was failing. The teacher strikes in the 80's affected extracurricular activities meaning that I didn't get to play rugby as much as I needed to become a professional player. I didn't get an interview with the Army Air Corps at Sandhurst because of my social background. All these excuses may have some truth behind them but I could have overcome them all had I really wished to. Had I taken responsibility for myself.

Whilst the environment undoubtedly has some effect on an individual it cannot be the sole reason as some people strive on regardless. A friend of mine supports an orphanage in West Africa. The children there have come from appalling backgrounds: many have been abused, discarded and left to fend for themselves. On one visit I was as delighted as my friend to hear that one of the eldest had just been accepted to university to study accountancy. There are those whose character will allow them to succeed in any given circumstance, which is fantastic but not really my point. My point is that actually many people possess that character, that drive to succeed but at times it seems to lie dormant, as it did in me. As a Leader it is possible for you to wake this ability by encouraging, inspiring and showing that we are all responsible for own actions and that we can achieve despite the environment we find ourselves in. Leaders are there to assist in the development of their team; sometimes merely showing that you believe they can develop and giving them the responsibility to do so is sufficient for them to flourish.

We all have certain beliefs. Our beliefs frame reality in our own subjective view. We have beliefs about the world we live in, about the people in that world; we even have beliefs about beliefs. Most importantly we have beliefs about ourselves and sometimes these are what limit our development. Limiting beliefs can form in an instant and last a lifetime, if not challenged. They can be the reason so many people do not realise their potential. For some it is a teacher or parent who mentions that you are not able to do something and we believe it, for others perhaps an event where we try something that is not well received and the sense of failure is sufficient to ensure we never try it again. I believe that these beliefs were all formed from a positive intention; your unconscious mind devised a protective measure to avoid you being put in an uncomfortable situation again, it makes it so nerve-wracking that you will not attempt whatever it is. The good news is that these limiting beliefs can be overcome; they can be changed. If one of your staff has been told over and over that they could never amount to anything, then by telling them that you believe that they can and supporting them on their journey, you can assist them to change that belief. Why is 'fire-walking' so popular in the world of personal development? It is not so that people know that if they should ever be caught in a situation when they have to traverse a path of burning embers on the one day that they have forgotten their shoes that they will be okay. It is because our beautiful minds can learn in an instant that if such a walk is possible then perhaps some of those other beliefs you had, that you did not think possible, you can actually overcome too.

A final word on getting to know your staff. I have already mentioned how we are all different but it really is worth re-emphasising the point. The loudest voice does not necessarily have the best answer. As a Leader it is up to you to allow your staff to be their best in their own way. Just because someone may appear shy and retiring to you that may not be the case. Some of us are just more introverted than others. Some like to work alone, have their own space and think better without distractions. Others crave crowded spaces and noise. The psychologist, Carl Jung first gave us the theory that people are either an introvert or an extrovert. Actually, he stated that we tend to be a bit of both but with most of us one side appears to be more dominant. Many businesses, including the military, have taken on a series of procedures for testing for psychological types along with psychological functions; you may have taken a Myers-Briggs Type Indicator assessment yourself? They do this as a guide to particular suitability to a specific role. Whilst the MBTI assessment indicates a certain personality, I do not believe that it actually determines your potential. I certainly did not fit the 'norm' when tested, more on that later.

If you have the opportunity to conduct the assessment on yourself or your staff then it can be an interesting exercise but do not then let it become a self-fulfilling prophecy. It is a guide, and a very good one, to your dominant personality; it does not mean that you are only capable of the 'suited career choices' that it may then recommend. The Myers & Briggs Foundation's own website, myersbriggs.org, highlights certain circumstances that can affect your results and encourages participants to engage more with the process in order to establish what they call your true type. Sadly, this fact is often omitted when a mass test is performed on a large group. It is sufficient to remember that we are not all the same and that we will benefit from treating people as the individuals that they are. We are context-based machines.

I have seen employees not sent on certain tasks because it was felt that they would be unable to restrain themselves and would end up saying the wrong thing at the wrong time. There are also examples of others being left out because of their lack of drive to be heard. It is worth remembering that many people do not want to be a Leader, do not want to move out of the role they already undertake only to find themselves spending more time supervising, not actually doing. Well, the world needs people like that too. It is up to the Leaders to recognise this, sometimes by just talking, and then ensure that their experience is not lost.

By getting to know your staff, you will soon find out who enjoys what and who works best under what circumstance. Of course, it does not mean that sometimes they will be required to step out of their comfort zone and partake in events that they would not choose to do. It does mean that you will be aware when such events are taking place and anticipate the need for extra support. As with most things in life, it is possible to keep it simple; ultimately treat staff how you would wish to be treated. You cannot really know them beyond what they are willing to share. It is equally important that we know ourselves and getting to do so will be the subject of the next chapter.

"Who are you?"

Points to Remember - Getting to Know Your Staff:

- Seek Inspiration over motivation.

- What do I know about my team?

- Everyone is different and needs to be treated as such.

- Rapport is vital to effective communication.

- Not talking is not 'not communicating'.

- How well someone works for you largely depends on how you approach them, which depends on how well you know them.

- Clarify understanding.

- Be positive and reward success.

- By pre-framing meetings, I can keep them on track.

- Be prepared to challenge limiting beliefs.

- Treat people how you would wish to be treated.

3

GETTING TO KNOW YOURSELF / YOUR SELF

*"Don't ask what the world needs,
ask what makes you come alive and go and do that.
Because what the world needs is
people who have come alive."*

Howard Thurman

How well do you know yourself? It is a serious question; I've emphasised the need to know one's staff and it is equally important to truly understand our Self. What is clear about the successful Leaders of the world is the undeniable passion they possess for their goals. I have mentioned the infectious nature of listening to someone speak who is passionate about their topic. A Leader that is passionate about their goals, the goals of the business and those personnel involved in the business demonstrates this infectious quality daily. The example you set really can be the best source of inspiration to others. We need to understand what we value most, what makes us tick, to ensure we are getting the best from ourselves.

Can you take a moment to ask yourself a few questions? What is your passion? What is it that you do that really makes you come alive? What would you do if money was no object, if you had all you needed, what would you do because you want to? There are a lot of Leaders in the world that are doing just that. They are doing it because they love doing it, whatever it is. That drive to succeed in their chosen field is inspiring to those around them. There are many talented people in the world but talent alone just isn't enough to make it where you want to be. Passion and drive, a willingness to keep going, overcoming setbacks and demonstrating to yourself and others just how much you care is key. How passionate are you about your current role? If you aren't then how can you possibly expect others to be? This does not necessarily mean a change of career is required although that may be the case. What can be done that would make you passionate about your work?

Srully Blotnick, an author and psychologist, conducted a 20-year study to establish how millionaires make their money. In 1960 his studies categorised 1500 business students into two groups. Group A consisted of those who said they wanted to make money first so they could do what they really wanted to do later, after they had taken care of their financial concerns. In Group A there were 1245 graduates, 83% of those studied. The remaining 255 graduates in Group B were going to pursue their true interests first, sure that money would eventually follow. In 1980, of the 1500 graduates, 101 were now millionaires. 1 graduate came from Group A and 100 came from Group B. Now I am not saying that being millionaires meant that they were successful, happy, had a fantastic sense of wellbeing or anything else but it is an interesting result considering they were business students and often making money is an indication of how successful a business is.

"It's hard to tell with these Internet startups if they're really interested in building companies or if they're just interested in the money.

I can tell you, though: If they don't really want to build a company, they won't luck into it. That's because it's so hard that if you don't have a passion, you'll give up."

Steve Jobs

We tend to go that extra mile for something we believe in, something we want to do. The things we enjoy doing we like to do more often and we get better at doing them. It seems that most people's definition of success revolves around how much money they make. I see this so often when someone has spent years working their arse off to make money to do the things they think they want only to find that wasn't what they wanted all along. Leaders generally have a distinct ideal of what success will look like to them. I always like to clarify my mission success criteria before I begin, otherwise how will I know when I have achieved what I set out to do? How will you know when you have succeeded? What will be the indication of success?

Take a moment to dream, how will you know when you have fulfilled your dream? What is your mission success criteria? What will it mean to you and your team? I often hear of so-called motivational speakers and coaches alike who chastise the dreams of those in their charge. The most common reason being that it's not realistic. Well, what is realistic and what is possible for you? Look up from your book now and just look around for a moment. How many man-made objects can you see in your surroundings? How many were there? Too many to count I imagine. How many achievements of mankind can you think about, what can you see in the various media windows to another world on offer to you right now. The truth is everything man-made, or woman made, or however you choose to identify for that matter, came from a thought, a dream that to many other people might have been unrealistic. As a young man if Neil Armstrong had said he dreamed of walking on the Moon he may have been chastised. If Bill Gates or Steve jobs had said to you as a teenager, I dream of being one of the most influential people in the world, what would you have said? What would your response have been to a geeky teenager if he told you he had dreamed of being a billionaire before he was 25? Mark Zuckerberg did become a billionaire that young, although I don't think the money was the driving force. I am sure a young Kate Middleton, like a lot of young girls, dreamed of being a Princess. Just 18 months after seriously damaging his back in a parachuting accident, Bear Grylls became the youngest Briton ever to summit Everest, who'd have believed it possible? Whatever the dream for you or those around you, as a Leader you are there to assist in making them happen. Dreams change of course as our priorities change also. I used to dream of living somewhere sunny now my dream is living closer to my daughter. Once she is grown up perhaps the lure of the sun will return, who knows? Frank Sinatra once said, well he sang, "some people get their kicks stomping on a dream". Don't be that person, be the one who listens to the dream and guides and supports, by doing this the person whose dream it is will work out how realistic it may be. Help to overcome the limiting beliefs we discussed in the previous chapter.

The whole point of these dreams or goals is that it ignites inspiration. It puts us in a proactive, positive frame of mind. We may well find that enroute to such a dream another dream takes priority, so what? When situations change, I change my mind, what do you do? The object is not to be consumed by the future or the past but to act in the now and whatever puts us in the right frame of mind to do that can only be a good thing. As a Leader it is up to us to ensure not only that we are in the right frame of mind but also that those we lead are too. 'Encouraging' is one tool we have to do this.

When we achieve a goal then it is important to find another one. As someone who achieved his childhood dream pretty early in life, there was then a period of anticlimax for me as I deliberated over the journey I had taken. It would have been very easy for me to stagnate and go no further. Instead, I made new goals and took from the experience the important lesson that I, personally, need multiple goals. I have spent a lot of time over the years mulling over my next goal with varying degrees of success. Without doubt the goals that I am less satisfied with were because I had been less specific with the final outcome. When it comes to work, I have learnt that I would rather earn less doing something I enjoy than work in an area that doesn't satisfy me. At times the results I had been aiming for just weren't ecologically right for me. The basis of the results had either been materialistic or else I hadn't thought through the consequences. As an example, I have had many houses but not since childhood have I actually had somewhere I would call a home, until very recently. What is interesting to me is the house I now call a home, unlike the others that I owned, I rent so the structure itself isn't even mine.

My passion from a very young age was that I wanted to be a military pilot. Hardly headline news is it? - 'Boy wants to be a pilot when he grows up.' There are many people who would argue that you can't do both! For me flying was all that mattered. Somehow, I would achieve my goal. I just didn't believe the teachers and other well-intentioned advisors that encouraged me to pursue a more 'achievable' career. I had made my decision and was committed to seeing it through. I wasn't put off by the rejection from the Royal Air Force or the one from the Fleet Air Arm, not even the rejection from the Army Air Corps whilst already undertaking Officer Training at the Royal Military Academy Sandhurst. I was passionate about flying and truly believed it was for me. I had cared

Getting to Know Yourself / Your Self

enough to join the Air Cadets when 13 years old and learn all I could about flying. I had flown solo in a glider and a light aircraft and whenever asked what I would be doing with my life, would answer quite definitely that I would be a pilot; I believed it too. Looking back now I am amazed that I kept at it for so long under such opposition. The reason I am sure is that I didn't dwell for a second on the negative responses; I drew from the positive support from my parents and others that offered encouragement as it matched my belief. During my inevitable flying career in the Army Air Corps, I would always look for the next role that I could really care about. The roles I really believed in that would allow me to share that belief with those I was leading. An officer's career is supposedly mapped out on a pathway to becoming a General. Of course not everyone wants to be in the Army long enough to become a General and so certain stepping-stones become irrelevant. I actually had to sign letters stating that I was potentially career fouling myself to take the posts that I did. I have no regrets. I had a wonderfully fulfilling Army flying career that included a tour with the Fleet Air Arm and even flying in the RAF Role Demonstration at air shows throughout the country, though thankfully in an Army Air Corps Apache. Why did I leave the Army? Because I developed a new passion.

"All men dream, but not equally. Those who dream by night, in the dusty recesses of their mind, wake to find it was all vanity. But the dreamers of the day are dangerous, for they may act their dreams with open eyes and make things happen."

T.E. Lawrence

I cannot encourage you enough to take the time to really find out about yourself. Ask yourself those searching questions: What do I really enjoy doing? What makes me tick? What am I truly passionate about? What is important about these things to me? How do I know when I have succeeded? There are many more questions of course and also many ways in which you can be sure of your chosen direction. I would advise using a coach to assist you. Not just because I am one, although that would be a good reason, I am sure, but a good coach will allow you to see what is best for you without telling you or judging you. Be careful though, there are some bad coaches, do your homework first. I am happy to help find someone suitable. My contact details are at the end of this book. Don't be fooled by the business versus life coach aspect, anyone who thinks there is a difference is either working in the wrong business or living the wrong life. When you discover what it is that you really care about you will find it so much easier to lead others on that same path. Once you know what it is that you want to do then make that decision to commit. My good friend, Mike Weeks, now a very successful 'change agent', made a decision one day to become a rock climber. Not just any old climber though, he decided to undertake free climbing, without ropes. In order to ensure his commitment, he would tell everyone willing to listen of his intentions. This level of commitment he cites as a catalyst in ensuring he achieves his goals. The most obvious reason I can find for not achieving something in the past is that I was not totally committed to the task.

I mentioned in the last chapter, the Myers Briggs Type Indicator assessment and how I did not fit the norm. When I took the assessment, I was already an Officer in the Army and a qualified helicopter pilot. On seeing the result, the assessor said quite sincerely, "If we had been conducting this a few years ago and you had taken this during selection, you wouldn't even be here!" Now, I have no idea if he was indeed serious and I wasn't about to ask any more questions for fear of what it might mean. Unlike everyone else in the room, my result had been that I was an introvert. The full result, for those familiar with the assessment was INTJ, Introvert-iNtuition-Thinking-Judgement. The only aspect that the assessor focused on was that everyone else was an extrovert and I was not. How could I have got into the role I now found myself? At the time it bothered me, it doesn't now-well not much bothers me now. With the limited information offered to us, it appeared I should have been a scientist or a librarian, which at least raised a laugh in the crew-room. That is the trouble with only an insight to a theory and not the whole story. It was not until years later that I was able to study a full profile for an INTJ and it makes a lot of sense to me. Incidentally, in my experience I have witnessed a number of people that would likely be labelled introverts handle the excitement of a war zone as well as the excitement of a boardroom extremely admirably, so be sure to understand these assessments before acting on them. The psychological writer, Susan Cain released her book, Quiet. The Power of Introverts in a World That Can't Stop Talking. I hope the assessor who took my MBTI reads it. I am not saying introverts are better than extroverts or making a judgement about any personality traits. What I am saying is that in the same way it helps to get to know your staff, it is vital to get to know yourself, or as Jung might put it, your Self. Knowing your strengths and weaknesses is really important and being able to use or compensate for them as you build your self-awareness will assist you as a Leader.

There are some companies that are using psychometric testing to such an extreme that they are filling their offices, workforce or aircraft with personnel whose results are almost identical. Whilst I see the advantage on perhaps not employing those at the ends of the spectrum, I also see a danger in having a group of people that supposedly think and act alike. Who will question an action, where is the variety of thought?

Whilst discussing testing, it is worth examining the many and varied tests and theories about leadership styles. Throughout the years since the first edition, I have continued to lead, study, and experience leadership. Maintaining my curiosity and keenness to learn, I completed a Masters in Organisational and Business Psychology. Whilst the dominance of the programme was about behavioural science, using the biopsychosocial model to further understand personal and organisational development, the underpinning thread was leadership and its importance in any business. Much has been written about various theories and styles of leadership and it can be confusing and somewhat daunting for many as they begin the journey to becoming a Leader, particularly those starting out and those stepping up from middle management.

A simple Google search will highlight the issue; it will return a plethora of contradictory headlines. 'The top 6 leadership theories', 'what are the five leadership theories?', '10 major leadership theories', '8 leadership styles you must know' and '20 types of leadership models and theories'. Where do you begin? Well, my hope is that through reflection, you will be able to come to your own conclusions about the academic information on offer. It is definitely worth studying the research and searching for examples that might help you by providing a framework for experimenting with different approaches in the situations you might find yourself in. Looking at why past Leaders were successful, or not, can give you a valuable learning experience, however such insight will not provide a checklist of how to proceed. As we have already seen, context is everything. You are not that past Leader; you are a unique individual and constantly changing and adapting to the circumstances you find yourself in. You are not leading the same staff as those before you, and your staff are also affected by their own unique experiences. The current task is unlikely to be identical to a previous task; the number of independent variables involved will undoubtedly change the journey even to a familiar goal.

Some of the styles on offer, I am sure you have heard of: transformational, transactional, trait theory, functional, servant, visionary, laissez-faire and autocratic. As previously mentioned, there are even tests available to find out 'your leadership style'; as if one style will suit all situations. If you are lucky enough to have made a successful career approaching every situation in exactly the same way then good for you but it would certainly not have worked for me. With my experience and observation, I would suggest a flexible approach would serve you better. Ask yourself, 'what is the outcome I wish to have from this situation?' and 'what would be the best approach?' There are a couple of theories, contingency and situational, which highlight the need to adapt to the context, inevitably through adaptation one is using the most suitable from a variety of styles. I have used the term Intentional Leadership before for clients wishing to hear a label, perhaps I should have just used 'Secret Leadership' but that would have negated the point of sharing!

One thing I hope that will become evident throughout this book is my belief that Leaders are not just born but anyone has the potential to Lead. However, one of the earliest theories was 'The Great Man Theory', the hypothesis asserted that indeed Leaders were born and that individuals cannot be taught to be an effective Leader. Subsequently, many theories have argued against such a theory and evidenced the development of personnel. This is the world of academia and science; someone posits a theory with evidence and research and others attempt to repeat the theory. The lack of ability to repeat such a theory under the same conditions leads to contrary opinion and new theories. However, just because something works only once out of a hundred times does not mean that it doesn't work. We have explored the aspect of context throughout this book; leadership is not often conducted under laboratory conditions, unless you run a laboratory, I suppose! Remain curious and creative. Using The Leadership Secret will allow you to experiment.

Back to the subject of 'getting to know your Self', let us touch on the subject of health. It is important to remember that when you are a Leader other people depend on you so it is all the more vital to look after yourself. I am not saying we should all hit the gym every day because quite frankly that doesn't necessarily mean healthy anyway. What I am suggesting is that with this increased self-awareness you take the time to recognise what it is that keeps you healthy and you do it. It could be playing a competitive sport, running, swimming, cycling, walking, yoga, chi kung, meditation or whatever. The important thing is that you partake in something that you feel is good for you and you eat healthy too. Again, that is whatever food happens to be healthy for you. As there is a direct link between mind and body it is obvious that we need to keep both fit. (I appreciate that some of you may believe that the mind and body are one. If that is the case then that is fine, from an operating and explanation point of view it is easier to assume that they are separate although intrinsically linked. I see them as separate and to be blunt and simplistic with my own reasoning: one can retain an active mind within a paralysed body; equally one can have an active body but have lost control of their mind. Still, intrinsically linked.) Of the list of Leaders that you came up with earlier, how many of them look like they take care of themselves? I would imagine almost all of them. Inevitably, there are some Leaders that through misfortune succumb to illness and do not live long and fruitful lives and perhaps they serve as a reminder to be the best we can be right now.

"Here's to the crazy ones. The misfits. The rebels. The troublemakers. The round pegs in the square holes. The ones who see things differently. They're not fond of rules. And they have no respect for the status quo. You can quote them, disagree with them, glorify or vilify them. About the only thing you can't do is ignore them. Because they change things. They push the human race forward. While some may see them as the crazy ones, we see genius. Because the people who are crazy enough to think they can change the world, are the ones who do".

Apple Inc.

As I sat writing, the first edition of, this book in October 2011, the news that Steve Jobs, Apple's co-founder, had died began to dominate the headlines. When the newsreader announced his age, only 56, my stomach gave me that hollow sensation that it does when I am reminded of an unpleasant experience. 56 being the same age of my Dad when he had died 14 years earlier. As a great admirer of Steve Jobs, though saddened at his passing, I allowed a grateful and respectful smile to form as I looked around the room. I was typing on a MacBook Pro with my iPhone by my

THE LEADERSHIP SECRET

side. In its case was the iPad I had used in the previous day's meeting and on the table was an iPod docked neatly in a set of speakers. A passionate Leader who influenced millions and I include myself as one of those millions. Also, undoubtedly a man of courage, and it is courage that will be the subject of our next chapter.

Getting to Know Yourself / Your Self

Points to Remember - Getting to Know Your Self:

- What makes you come alive?

- If you want others to follow, make sure you believe in it first.

- Spend time setting your own goals.

- Understand your strengths and weaknesses and work on both.

- Stay as healthy as you can be.

- The people who are crazy enough to think they can change the world, are the ones who do.

4

A LEADER'S COURAGE

"Courage is not
*   the absence of fear,*
*   but rather the judgement that*
*   something else is*
*   more important than fear."*
Ambrose Redmoon

    One of the most nerve-wracking experiences a flying instructor can have, whilst on the ground, is the moment you send a student on their first solo flight. One can never be 100% certain of exactly how they will cope until you allow them the freedom to give it a go. At some point you have to have the courage to let go and let them fend for themselves. Once you do, they really fly.

    One attribute that every leader must possess is courage. Courage can be physical or moral. Physical courage on the battlefield is something I am well aware of and its effects on the morale of a unit are well documented throughout history. But what of courage away from the battlefield? As I have witnessed through coaching, for many people an enormous amount of courage is required just to stand up in front of others and speak and there are certain skills that we will cover later in the book under 'learning emotional state control' to assist with this. It also takes courage to delegate responsibility knowing that ultimately you will be the one held accountable. Everything is relative, so the fact that it requires physical courage to fly into an area of hostile fire simply does not matter at the point in time for the CEO who has to make a decision whether or not to lay off staff. Let's face it, most decisions a CEO has to make are difficult decisions, if it were easy then the chances are someone else would have already made it.

When responding to my first 'tic' (troops in contact) situation as a part of an Apache crew in Afghanistan, I was given a stark warning as I flew the aircraft within radio range of the unit under fire. Whilst giving us a situation report from the ground, the radio operator included his concern that it may be a trap set to shoot down the real intended target, us! He proceeded to relay intelligence conversations intercepted from the enemy, seemingly pleased that we were responding with Apaches, that this is what they were waiting for and that the 'big gun' was ready. The brave operator, having relayed this information, then asked if we will be continuing on the mission. Well, we had some pretty big guns too and a whole lot of training and preparation, and there was no way we were turning around whilst our fellow soldiers were under direct attack. I often reflect on the courage of that radio operator; he knew the serious nature of the predicament he and his unit were in, he knew that their best chance of extricating from the danger was through the top cover firepower that we were bringing, and yet he still passed on the warning and therefore the potential of being left to their own resources. We did manage to help them break contact, and on this occasion we didn't see the 'big gun' although another flight did destroy what could have been the weapon in question not long after.

It can take a lot of courage for a teenager to say 'no, I will not be part of a gang' or for the first person to stand up to a school bully. All are displays of physical courage and leadership in their own right. Moral courage can be a lot harder to display than the physical, especially as there is often more time to reflect on the consequences. It is about making decisions based on sound judgement - using the available information with a positive intention.

Moral courage is also about telling the truth when it comes to staff appraisals. What benefit are you offering someone by not informing them how they could improve? It is all about how you frame the conversation, as with meetings. If the goal is to provide constructive feedback in order for the subject to improve their own prospects of promotion and employability then you have a positive intention, right? Far too many people are afraid of feedback and far too many Leaders are afraid to give it. Do you think any athlete or sportsman who wants to be the best is afraid of feedback? Can you imagine Rafael Nadal saying to his coach, Uncle Tony, "don't tell me where I'm going wrong, I don't want to know." Of course, the coach also has to be able to know what is going wrong. I am reminded of an instructor I once had when learning to fly the Apache Helicopter who, after a pretty poor execution of a particular exercise by yours truly, simply said; "that was rubbish, do it better next time." What made it rubbish and what should I change to enable me to do it better next time? Thankfully there were others on hand eager enough to assist with my development!

My good friends, Daryll Scott and Ben Houghton, have written a brilliant book on this subject, Feedback or Criticism. With them I have been involved in workshops on the subject for managers in various businesses and it is quite apparent that it is a subject that many feel they need help with. As with all leadership, the crux of the matter is, do you care? Are you approaching it from a position of a positive intention? Is your aim to assist and develop? If this is the case then it is incumbent on you to make sure your member of staff knows that. If you are their Leader, they should see this in you every day. It may be that in your business the setup dictates that you are the Leader of some that you do not see very often, in which case you may need to spend a little more time pre-framing the discussion.

Imagine a situation where you are required to give someone feedback that you feel they may not like. We are concentrating here on a potentially negatively perceived trait as most Leaders don't have too much of an issue providing positive comments, although they may overlook doing so as we looked at in the chapter 'Getting to Know Your Staff'. Would it help to begin something like this? "I have some information about you that I feel is holding you back within this company. The thing is, I am certain that if you knew this information then you would be able to do something about it and in doing so would greatly improve your prospects of promotion. To be quite honest though, I am not sure how you are going to react to this information and it could be taken personally although I can assure you, my intention is only positive and to give you the chance to realise your potential. So, I could not tell you and allow you to carry on or I could discuss it with you and we can work together towards you gaining that promotion." Most of us are saying, just tell me, what is

A Leader's Courage

it, I assume? Those who really don't want to know have probably reached or exceeded their ceiling already. Look at what we've done though; we have stated our positive intention behind bringing up the issue. We have also offered support to the member of staff. Most of all we have given them the choice of receiving the information, so we are not merely telling, we are now responding to being asked. This is not purposely done for our benefit, although it does make it easier to deliver, it is done so our colleague is able to receive whatever the information is in a willing manner and therefore make an educated decision on their next action.

Moral courage is also required on the battlefield and to illustrate it I would like to share one of the most emotive moments from my career that provoked deep reflection and soul searching.

On a hot, dry day in Afghanistan in late 2006 an Afghan National Army convoy of infantry and their supporting vehicles was on a routine patrol through an area of known Taliban activity. The unit I was attached to had two Apache Attack helicopters in the area, both equipped with superb surveillance equipment, including infra-red and daylight cameras with an impressive 127 times magnification. They also carried multiple munitions: missiles, rockets and a 30mm chain gun capable of incredible accuracy and able to be sighted simply by the pilot looking at the selected target.

I was based at Camp Bastion assigned to the Immediate Response Team. The IRT was just that, an immediate response consisting of 2 Apache and two Chinook helicopters. Any sudden situation could see us scrambled immediately to provide support. Tasks varied from escorting a casualty evacuation Chinook to a 'pick up point' to a 'troops in contact' incident enabling an ambushed unit to continue the fight or extract. On this October day the IRT flight would be involved in both tasks.

As an instructor I was fortunate enough to be qualified to fly from both seats, front and rear (the Apache has a tandem cockpit). On this occasion I would sit in the rear and pilot for the Flight Commander, other times I would lead the patrol. It is often the case in aviation when the aircraft commander is of a lower rank than the pilot as it was today.

Through the crackle of our walkie-talkies came the call to scramble the IRT and pulses racing, along with the other pilot, J, I dashed across the dusty track, already sweating under the desert sun to ready my machine whilst the two commanders rallied at the operations tent to gain

THE LEADERSHIP SECRET

information about the mission. The ANA convoy had been attacked and had taken casualties. The IRT Chinook was being readied and one Apache would be used to escort it to and from the scene. Although our wingman would be taking the task I continued with the start as a spare just in case, it is only a big computer after all and sometimes the 'computer says no!' With, T on board they taxied for a swift departure, so I shut down and kicked my way back through the dust for a brief on the situation. The sombre mood in the tent did little to hide the seriousness of the incident unfolding. One of the worst nightmares in a place used to sleepless nights; hostages had been taken.

The two Apaches already at the scene were running low on fuel, so as soon as T and J returned, we were to head out as a pair and take over the supporting task. We used the transit time to listen to the various radio frequencies and build our own situational awareness. This isn't the book to go into detail, that one is coming, but in essence the hostages, two ANA soldiers had been located by our sister flight. The flight had offered accurate intelligence on the situation and was capable of formidable firepower but the Afghan commander on the ground had decided that a rescue would be too risky. Not wishing to endanger the rest of his men his decision was to extract to the relative safety of the open desert and leave the two behind.

We were all struggling with his decision - it was very alien to our armed forces and after many attempts to sway the commander it was clear he would not be changing his mind. On handover with the other flight, our wingman covered the extracting convoy whilst we concentrated on the hostages.

In the following minutes countless options were played through not only our minds but also through the minds of the various staffs of the various headquarters now involved, including that of the Brigade Commander. Suppressing the sickening feeling in my stomach, I watched as over 40 insurgents had gathered around the two kneeling, bound soldiers. We had made clear our presence to the armed gang but had stopped short of engaging at this stage for fear of what would happen to the hostages. They were either unaware of our capability or simply didn't care - who knows? They had the capability to hit us with their shoulder launched Rocket-propelled grenades and the belief that such a hit, whether or not they were subsequently killed by our wingman, would earn them reward within their world.

The nature of such an event and the current 'rules of engagement' had quickly removed any immediate decisions from us, as the implications of which could be felt across the country and beyond affecting the whole mission. The Brigadier himself would decide the outcome. Our task now was to provide accurate information along with our own educated opinions and responses. Time was running out. The terrain did not in any way suit a heli-borne air assault. The constant threat of the hostages being held at gunpoint meant that in a split second their life could be over.

The facts were that in the past hostages had been subjected to unspeakable treatment before ending up executed and paraded in a sick effort to torment others. Now surrounded by an armed, merciless gaggle, even a well-trained unit just metres away would be unlikely to be able to rescue them alive; and well-trained units were still miles away. Sadly, the best option 'right now' would probably be to deliver a missile right on top of the hostages, ending their suffering instantly and avoiding any more to come whilst at the same time removing from the battlefield many of those responsible for already documented atrocities. The 'right now' option vanished as a vehicle arrived and the hostages were bundled into the backseat and along with several captors it sped off into the maze of compounds and tracks.

The many sources of intelligence feeding into the senior commander's HQ allowed him to make his difficult and courageous decision. Feigning our departure, I then manoeuvred the aircraft for the optimum attack run whilst our wingman concurrently prepared for his engagement. When the dust settled, the outcome had spared the hostages a fate worse than death but sadly not death itself. It was an horrendous experience for all of us involved and one that I have relived many times since. I'll never be okay with it, but I'm okay enough because history had shown that the ending for the hostages could have been a lot worse. I took comfort in the knowledge that given a similar situation I would be spared torture and the enemy would lose an opportunity to use me as a symbol in a sick promotion. I took comfort in the knowledge that I had a Leader with the moral courage to make decisions no matter how difficult.

Now it is pointless to say, 'well no decision I make will ever be as tough as his'. Whilst that may be true, I would hope, whatever decision you have to make is relevant and important to you and your staff at that

time. It may be of some comfort to remember that other people have had to make the kind of decision in the past and will do in the future that actually is life and death; even so it is not necessarily the case for you now. Whatever the context, the same personal difficulties arise even if the severity of the consequences is different. We can all get clouded by emotion and consequence - so it is important to have a process that can give you the courage to act. Take from that decision and use in the future, how that decision was made. Ask yourself the following questions:
- What is my positive intention?
- Do I have all the facts?
- Do I have as many of the facts as I could possibly have?
- What would happen if I did X?
- What would happen if I did not do X?
- What would not happen if I did X?
- What would not happen if I did not do X?
- What about Y and Z?

The dilemma for Leaders is often not that the decision has to be made but that those it affects will not understand why the decision was made. You cannot please all the people all the time. Some may be unhappy with your decisions, let's face it some will be unhappy with some of your decisions. Leadership involves pre-empting such decisions and communicating your reasons where appropriate. Inevitably not everyone will understand but if you care to accept this, your respect should stand.

There are many different ways a helicopter can approach a landing zone; such is the flexibility when there is no need for a runway. In the Army I would clearly state my intentions to the crew moments before such an approach. Considering the wind direction, the power available, any obstacles, my field of view, the position of our troops, the position of any enemy, known enemy weapon characteristics, etc. It would only take seconds and would let everyone know of my thought process and give them the chance to interrupt the process before beginning the manoeuvre, should it be necessary, and would then allow them to get on with their own tasks without distraction.

Keep it fair. Do you take the time to articulate the reasons behind your decision-making? If there is one thing certain to excite and anger the vast majority of the human population it is an example of injustice. In every aspect of life, we have an incredible ability to deal with hardship, perhaps bad luck and even foul play. When it comes to an injustice though, you can be sure that there will be a rise out of someone. Think about it for a minute and you will find countless examples. When relationships breakdown the primary reason for prolonged ill feeling will be when one partner is seen to get more than the other. No one minds waiting in line until someone else jumps the queue. Supporters can accept their side losing an important match if beaten fair and square but include a dodgy decision by an official that just might have turned the game and that is a different story. National disputes and international conflicts alike have been born out of dispute about the disparity between the treatment of some over the treatment of others. Yes, there are some that accept logic easier than others but that to them is being fair, that thought process is their idea of justice.

Every one of us is acutely aware of the impact the feeling of injustice can have on the human psyche. So as a Leader make sure you believe your decisions to be fair. That does not mean that difficult decisions will not have to be made or that some should not benefit from their work over others. Have the thought in the back of your mind when making these decisions, in your opinion, is this fair? Can you justify it? Incentives for good work and added bonuses for promotion can be a good thing; they give people a reason to want to further themselves in your company. When you really get to know your staff, you will know who values what kind of incentive. By understanding what motivates and inspires an individual, one is able to tailor any form of reward.

Underestimate the power of perceived injustice at your peril. I have seen when bad feeling enters an organisation and it takes a long time for it to leave. Ensuring that you apply The Leadership Secret will not only ensure that you remain fair with your decisions but the empathy you feel will also highlight any decisions beyond your control that your staff may feel are unfair. Often it can be a case of misunderstanding and not seeing the full picture. In these cases, it is the Leader that will investigate solutions and provide explanations working with their staff, avoiding a 'them and us' situation that so many organisations seem unable to shake. Naturally there will be times when confidentiality or intellectual property rights preclude your freedom to explain your thought process fully. In these instances, the trust you have developed amongst your staff will see you through.

THE LEADERSHIP SECRET

Since writing the first edition of this book, I spent a few years as a commercial helicopter pilot. The flying included flying privately for the Royal Family, corporate flying, and a couple of years flying HEMS (Helicopter Emergency Medical Services). One of the most difficult aspects of flying helicopters as a job is telling people when you can't fly. It takes courage to say no, whatever the reason. Although I never wanted to let them down or those waiting to receive them, The Royal Family are very aviation aware and were very understanding on the odd occasion that the weather curtailed a flight. With sufficient notice, a backup plan would swing into action with little disruption. Corporate clients vary the most in their response. There are conflicting interests here; a pilot is unlikely to be paid if they don't fly, often corporate clients are extremely wealthy, used to getting what they want and are not used to not getting their way. Many of them are unaware of the regulations and real safety implications and, having purchased a very capable 'all weather' aircraft, don't like to accept that just because it can do it, it does not mean the law allows it. The expectation of being dropped wherever, whenever often outweighs reality. Another aspect is the belief that all pilots are capable of flying anywhere, at any time in any weather; this is not the case. Military flying is often at the extremes of the aircraft and crew performance but calculated risks are taken and a great deal of training undertaken in preparation, it is rarely on a whim. Sadly, even experienced military aviators have been caught out when flying commercially succumbing to the pressures, either real or implied. Saying no when flying a HEMS helicopter could clearly be a difficult task as someone needs help. The regulations are generally well within the capability of the experienced pilots and aircraft, for good reason. However, a bad decision could mean making an already bad situation a lot worse. It could also affect the whole of the country's HEMS capability if prevalent rule breaking required further scrutiny. Remember no one likes unwanted surprises, especially in the heat of the moment, so I would always ensure that the doctors and paramedics were well briefed at the start of each duty on any potential for a 'no go' that day. The professionalism of the medical crews was such that this was very rarely an issue, and when it was overly frustrating for them, it was only because they cared.

We have seen how important it is for a Leader to show courage in a variety of situations. In order to overcome the fear, we need to be in control of our own emotional state. In the next chapter we examine what that entails and how to achieve such desired control.

"Courage is treating fear as a reminder to Switch Focus."

THE LEADERSHIP SECRET

Points to Remember - Courage:

- Courage is finding something more important that fear.

- When providing feedback, it will be easier when I state my positive intention and agree the frame of the discussion.

- It is the responsibility of leaders to make decisions.

- When making decisions, I will ask:

- What is my positive intention?

- Do I have all the facts?

- Do I have as many of the facts as I could possibly have?

- What would happen if I did X?

- What would happen if I did not do X?

- What would not happen if I did X?

- What would not happen if I did not do X?

- What about Y and Z?

- I will anticipate whether my decisions could be misunderstood.

5

LEARNING EMOTIONAL STATE CONTROL

"If you can
keep your head
when all about you
are losing
theirs..."

Rudyard Kipling, 'If'

Do you know anyone that in their own special field comes across as super intelligent and yet they don't seem to possess any commonsense? They undoubtedly have a higher-than-average intelligence quotient, IQ, and yet are unable to impart their knowledge. They may even work extremely well and productively but perhaps only in isolation and not as a part of the team. More and more businesses have become aware of the need to look further than IQ with regards to their employees and are becoming more aware of EQ, Emotional Quotient or, EI Emotional Intelligence to give it its more common name. It is suggested that the first published use of the term emotional quotient was in 1987 in an article by Keith Beasley in MENSA Magazine. In 1990 psychologists Peter Salovey and John Mayer followed up with their article 'emotional intelligence' in the Journal: Imagination, Cognition, and Personality. Popularity of the concept grew with the 1996 publication of the book 'Emotional Intelligence: Why it can matter more than IQ', by Daniel Goleman. An emotionally intelligent Leader understands the importance of developing their interpersonal skills. They utilise the skills and develop their team whilst achieving the goals. EI allows them to control their own emotional state, to keep their head when others are losing theirs, to make seemingly rational decisions during a crisis and avoid the 'emotional hijack' that we often witness in people who cannot cope.

Have you heard people use the phrase "I just couldn't think straight" when describing how they reacted to an emotionally upsetting event? Well, the chances are they actually couldn't. Our emotional memory is stored in a part of the brain called the limbic system and within the limbic system is an almond sized portion called the amygdala, actually there are two, a left and a right. Our amygdala is our first port of call for a reaction to information received from our senses and provokes in us emotional feelings such as fear, love, lust, excitement and many more.

The reactions caused by the amygdala are instant for a very good reason, indeed our own survival. It is this powerful emotional response, able to override any rationale that enables amongst other things what some term the fight or flight response. For human beings to have survived on this planet for so long and evolved as we have, at least some of us, our distant ancestors required an inbuilt ability to escape from potentially life-threatening experiences automatically without delay. Many wild beasts roamed the land and if encountered there would have been no time for discussion, only action. This response of course is still just as important today if for very different reasons. If while crossing the road a vehicle seemingly appears from nowhere, we tend not to think about it too much before jumping out of the way. We have learned throughout life from our own experiences and that of others that should a vehicle come in contact with ourselves at speed it is likely to hurt quite a lot and so we do our best to avoid it. This is why we spend time and effort educating our children on the dangers of the road to build in the immediate response. It is more accurate to say that we possess a fight, flight or freeze response and it is the freeze response that needs eradicating. Incidentally for some people in complete control of their emotions they may, in the same instant, be able to focus, use foresight and fix the problem without fighting, taking flight or freezing; too many 'f's'? Semantics really, you cannot reason with a vehicle.

EI is not about extinguishing emotion, having emotion is vital to human evolution and is a sign of intelligence. Fear keeps us away from danger, love drives us to care for one another and grief reminds us what is

Learning Emotional State Control

important to us. EI is about recognising emotions and choosing your suitable reaction. Take anger as an example. Anger can be the most powerful of emotions and can lead to dramatic and damaging results. Can you think of a time when you were angry and your subsequent behaviour did little to help the situation? I can, it is a little embarrassing, isn't it? And yet much of the good that is done in the world is because someone got angry and decided to make a change. One event that springs to mind is Live Aid. Seeing the pictures of the starving in Ethiopia a man got angry. He was angry that such an event could happen in this so-called civilised world in the mid 1980s. He was angry that whilst Europe was allowing butter-mountains to go to waste a part of Africa was literally dying due to famine. Channeling his anger, Bob Geldof, now Sir Bob, arranged for the rock and popstars of the generation to come together to make a record, yes, a record, how old am I? No iTunes then! And hold concerts in the UK and USA televised around the world. His anger and subsequent action saved countless lives.

Acting on strong emotion is not necessarily a bad thing; it is how you react that counts. It is the ability to 'control yourself' that is key to success. I like the term 'State Control' when relating to one's own emotional state. To exercise State Control, it helps to learn State Understanding and State Awareness. I was sharing experiences one day with Ben Collins, The Stig from BBC's Top Gear. I was obviously keen to hear his driving exploits and he my flying exploits. Although, he was more interested in my work on state control, emotional state. He wondered when I first realised that remaining calm and controlled was so important to leading under pressure situations and of course how I do it? The state we find ourselves in directly affects our behaviour and actions. We will go into the how shortly as well as going onto how anyone can also learn this essential leadership trait but following Ben's question, I asked myself the same thing.

In my early 20's as a young 2nd Lieutenant I was lucky enough to command a troop of over 70 soldiers, the Combat Support Troop. Our main responsibility was the movement of combat supplies: ammunition, fuel, rations and other immediate requirements. We deployed to the former republic of Yugoslavia in December 1995. Actually, although we were on standby, we were told of our deployment on Christmas Eve and deployed on Boxing Day, two days later. I had already passed selection and been *loaded onto a pilots' course by this time but my Commanding Officer had personally asked me to delay the course and deploy with my troop as he did not want to have to change their leadership at this crucial stage. How could I refuse?*

During the 6-month tour I could not have been prouder of my Troop. They had to contend with atrocious driving conditions, the temperature was often below -30° Celsius, and the roads were in a poor state to say the least. The mapping was limited and to top it off there were still some of the warring factions out to kill them. The roads were often mined and snipers patrolled some areas. When you are driving a tanker containing many thousands of litres of fuel, some idiot taking pot shots at you can seriously ruin your day.

Towards the end of our time in Bosnia I was driving to the Regimental Headquarters, with my second in command, for an orders group with the senior staff. Only a couple of miles from our destination, the common occurrence of a road accident had caused a lengthy tailback. Unusually, we were waved through without discussion and as we crested the small hill it was clear why. My heart skipped a beat as I recognised one of my trucks in a ditch on the far side of the road. The impact had clearly been excessive as the load straps had snapped and the supplies were scattered around the vehicle. Military police, already on the scene, had cordoned off a badly damaged saloon car that sat in the middle of the road. The driver of the truck, Terry was nowhere to be seen. I could feel myself heat up and my pulse increase as the police explained the events, as they knew them; the truck had crested the hill and rounded the bend as a civilian saloon car with a male driver, female front seat passenger and child in the rear cornered in the opposite direction. The saloon car unfortunately was in the middle of the road leaving no room for the truck to pass. Both drivers took avoiding action but still collided killing the female passenger instantly and injuring the other occupants. The truck continued off the road where it impacted the ditch. Both civilians had been taken to hospital in an ambulance and Terry had been taken to the nearest base, our intended destination with suspected severe head injuries. Sadly, the gruesome scene was all too familiar in this war-torn country.

We continued at best speed to the base to establish Terry's condition. I desperately sought an update from my colleagues and asked the medical staff if they needed anything. They did, a CASEVAC (casualty evacuation) and fast. The helicopter Immediate Response Team (IRT) was based at the field hospital about 15 minutes flying time away and so should surely be here any minute. My enquiries with the HQ staff did not fill me with the confidence that all was being done to expedite the required CASEVAC and I emphasised the need to rush. I was running from the operations room to the treatment room to the front gate ensuring that all was in place for when the helicopter arrived. Eventually the reassuring sound of the helicopter's rotor blades could be heard and the medical staff prepared Terry for the journey. At one corner of the stretcher, I assisted with carrying my injured soldier out of the base and through the dusty downwash; taking great care as we loaded him into the open side door and awaiting aircrew. The sense of responsibility could not have been stronger. One of the lives I was there to watch over appeared at that stage to hang precariously in the balance. As I watched the green and white striped helicopter lift and disappear over the hills, I thought I'd never see him again.

"When a soldier is at war, his mind should be at peace."
Lord Moran

One of the most common experiences of a sudden loss of state control is 'road rage'. For those who get road rage I would invite you to conduct an experiment. If you are one of those who thinks that everyone on the road who drives slower than them is an idiot and everyone that drives faster than them is a maniac then this may help. Next time someone races up behind you on the motorway, obviously wishing to overtake even though there is more traffic ahead and they will get nowhere, instead of raging, choose a different option. When safe to do so, change lanes and allow them to pass before regaining your position in the chosen lane with them now ahead. Whilst conducting your manoeuvre run through your mind possible permutations of why someone would be driving so badly? To get you going: They may have someone injured in the car and are trying to get them to hospital. Perhaps there is a pregnant woman in the back. They are late for a very important meeting. They are late for their wedding. They have left the oven on. Perhaps they are just a bad driver, in which case I would rather they were in front where I can avoid them than behind me where they have to avoid me. How about thinking of some reasons that would cause you to drive in such a way. For those with kids this is easy for starters, any reason that could be threatening to them. The truth is we have no idea why they are driving so poorly and we are merely guessing a reason. The time it takes to conduct the mental exercise described will be sufficient for the event to pass by in a much less eventful manner and allow them to drive to a different scene of their accident, one which does not include you.

As an example, let me explain a scenario I found myself in. Close to where I once lived is a road junction where a single lane, from the left, joins a double lane, from the right, to form three lanes on a one-way system. Very soon after this join is a left turn, which means those driving in the original two-lane section now need to come further left should they choose to turn left up ahead. The junction is further complicated by the fact that it is on a corner and flanked by shops, which although double yellow lined inevitably means that someone has parked alongside, idiot! Just kidding, I'm calm. On this occasion I was travelling in the left lane and all lanes were fairly busy. A person in a Mercedes, obviously, joining from the right was aggressively trying to push in front of my car although he was still not clear of my front wheels. At the same moment I began braking to let him in he decided to brake too, clearly not happy with the split second that he had been unable to change lanes. This meant that his car for a while became level with me, allowing the occupant to hurl expletives through the open windows at me. Why do people do that to absolute strangers? Anyway, I merely shrugged and asked what I was supposed to do under the circumstances, too calm for his liking. His continued braking took him to behind my car where he decided an equally aggressive cut-in before the car behind me would do the trick. Unfortunately, he was anything but cool and so misjudged his manoeuvre clipping the rear corner of my car as he turned. Still shouting expletives as he exited his, not quite so pristine now, Merc, I climbed out to inspect the damage. I immediately matched his body language striding towards him and then simply asked why did he do that [hit my car]?

Breaking my stride as I approached him, I calmly walked between the cars and reached in to my pocket for my phone. His excitement was slowly subsiding as I took a few photos of the damage to both cars and then asked for his details. By this time, realising he was getting no shouting match or worse from me, he began to speak with a little more fluency although still physically shaking. Clearly his fault, I commented that these things happen and that 'I'm sure we can sort it out.' With details exchanged he apologised and we went on our way. When we met a few days later for him to recompense me he again apologised profusely and thanked me for being so understanding, making a point of how decent I had been. Well, I did it for my benefit. What would I have gained by continuing the verbal abuse or escalating it to physical? Nothing but more trouble. I couldn't change that he had hit my car. I couldn't even change that the fact he had hit my car pissed me off. What I could change was how to react to the emotional response of being angry about him hitting my car and his reaction to doing so. It takes two to argue and one to decide it's over.

Let us examine what controls our emotional state: very simply it is the product of whatever we are currently thinking, our internal representation, and our current physiology. It is a mind-body experience. The term 'internal representation' is very useful in explaining our thoughts because what we think at any given moment is given meaning based on our life of experience. Everything we have ever experienced is stored in our mind, imagine a vast library of information, a go-to reference point unique to each of us. This library not only contains information about our experiences but it is able to link these experiences to one another in order to give us an immediate response to a given situation. It is continually updating as new data is loaded through our senses, all of this is an automatic action of our unconscious.

For example: We see an object, our unconscious scans our library and based on the image, referenced against past experience, it identifies the object as a car. The library is able to generalise; the car is a means of transport, and specify; the car is an Aston Martin (I know blatant endorsement, do you think they'll give me one?). In the first edition, I stated that our conscious attention is able to handle 5-9 items at any given moment. This means that although we have a vast library, only 5-9 books can be out at any one time. Subsequent research is challenging this, and suggestions are now that the short-term memory, which we are using in this situation, is capable of up to 4 items. The good news is our unconscious has continued access to the library and so is able to react to threatening situations. Additionally, it is worth noting that new experiences can affect past memories, so in the library analogy it is as if a conscientious librarian is constantly editing the vast library. There is still a great deal of research and peer review being conducted in this area, and it highlights the constant challenge and development of scientific research.

In any given moment, using this library, our mind is able to attribute meaning to a situation. This meaning is then represented as our thoughts in terms of our voice in our head, imagined images or memories. We are all aware of the various emotional states that we find ourselves in from time to time and we give them labels in terms of language in order to give them meaning: happy, angry, sad, determined, tired, excited, etc. We have decided on these labels based on those individual life experiences stored in our internal library. A common misconception about our various states is that we are not able to bring them under our conscious control, that we find ourselves in them due to what is happening to us and that they are only ever an automatic response created by our unconscious. Firstly, an identical event can happen to many different people and they can all end up experiencing a different emotion because of it. Secondly, an identical event can happen to us separated by time and our own individual reaction will be different. So, it is not the event itself that causes our state but the importance or meaning that we give it at that time. For a lot of us, yes until we raise our awareness of 'emotional state control', i.e., bring it to our conscious attention it does appear to be an automatic response that we have no control over but, as we will see, this too can be overcome.

Let us look at the response to an event situation. A work colleague tells a joke to the team during a meeting. Some of the team laugh, others are offended as they considered it rude, some don't get the joke, others are not offended but they didn't think it was very funny. The point is, it is not what the colleague says that causes our reaction but the meaning we give it. Two people ride the very same roller-coaster; one was petrified and will never ride it again, the other thought it was great and wants another go. Have you ever seen a movie? I am sure you have, and does your opinion of the film always match everyone else's you know? I am sure it doesn't. Everything is relative, relative to our own self, and more than that, relative to our own self in the moment. I like to eat ice-cream on the beach when it is a warm sunny day not when it is -2° Celsius and blowing a gale. It is an addition to the theory of relativity. Rather than how we view something externally, how we view something internally, in our mind.

Learning Emotional State Control

Shall we take a moment to discuss our mind? Rather importantly I like to remember that my mind, unconscious or conscious is 'me'. Therefore, if my mind is creating a response to any given situation then it does so from a position of positive intention for my wellbeing, however it may appear. Until we accept this and understand that we can still communicate with our unconscious reactions in order to override them we will forever be out of control. Often a phobic response is created as a result of a single learned experience. That is amazing is it not? How powerful is the brain to learn something in an instant and then be able to run that same pattern forever after? Except there is a glitch isn't there with regards to phobias, in that the reaction rarely suits the cause? In fact, the very definition of a phobia is that it is an irrational response. What is even more incredible is that often the sufferer of the phobia is consciously aware and able to converse about how irrational it is and yet unable to override their own reaction.

Let us briefly go back to our example of a car and how based on the information stored in our internal library of experience, our mind is able to link all relevant information and correctly identify what we see as a car. How this image is represented is then based on this stored information. The car in question could look like a friend's car and perhaps a thought of that friend will enter your mind, it could be the model of your first car and maybe images of you at an earlier age will come up. For some it could be identical to a car that they were involved in an accident with, and thoughts of an unpleasant situation can occur. All different examples of how we create meaning to a situation based on our past experience, how this meaning is then represented and then how these thoughts affect our current emotional state. In the latter example of an unpleasant situation being relived it can lead to post traumatic stress. As they are just products of our own mind, we are able, with practice, to re-programme how the links are made and attribute new meaning.

I was working with a friend of mine, Mel on a management development course he was running for a telecoms company. He happened to mention to the group that I had done some work with assisting with ridding phobias and one of the ladies asked for my help. It turned out that for as long as she could remember she was unable to turn on a shower. She could get into a shower and turn off a shower but could not bring herself to turn one on, and understandably it was an issue for her as well as for her husband who was forever called on to turn it on. She had no idea where this had developed from and it didn't matter because clearly it was real for her. It is conceivable that she may have turned one on as a child and the water may have given her enough of a shock, too hot, too cold or too powerful, for her unconscious to step in and from then on protect her from a repeat experience, who knows? The fact was that the kind of protection provided by her unconscious, whatever the positive intention behind it, was no longer required. Thankfully I was able to assist her and she got rid of her phobia in just 15 minutes. The New Code Neurolinguistic Programming (NLP) techniques employed are more suited to another book, suffice to say that it was merely an exercise in allowing the mind to create a different response rather than run an automatic pattern. Using the mind's ability to associate a context with an imagined or recalled metaphor and creating the conditions for the client to experience a different state whilst in the same context was key. This appears to interrupt the recurring problem state sufficiently for the mind to have a choice of state in the future. Contact me if you wish to know more.

So, the important issue with regards to our emotional state is, what are you running in your mind? What are you visualising? What sounds are you hearing? What is that little voice inside you saying? (That little voice is still you, by the way, and contrary to what some believe it is on your side). If you walk to a meeting and on the way all you can think of is how no one will like your proposal, how they will laugh at you and that they just will not understand your point, is that the best preparation? We can easily experience how internal representation affects our state. Do you have a favourite song? If so, then play it in your head, how does it make you feel? Can you remember a time in your life when something made you laugh? A film, a show, a friend? For those of you that are married can you remember the moment you were proposed to, or you proposed and the moment you or they said yes? How does it make you feel when you remember these different events? You can imagine things too; what would it be like to win millions on the lottery? Seeing the effect of how a child's state is seemingly controlled by what they are thinking shows what we go through, only for a child it is in quick time. 'I'm hungry-make some noise, no response-cry, food arrives, I'm curious, it doesn't look right, refuse it-get angry, throw it away-cry, okay I'll try it, I like it-smile, I'm happy-laugh.' Children are able to flit from one state to another in a second; it is when we dwell on these inner thoughts that our state can intensify, which can be a negative or indeed an incredible positive.

When my daughter was four, like all four-year-olds she was scared of a few things: the dark, going underwater, people dressed as big pink dinosaurs who walk around shopping centres, and Captain Hook from Peter Pan, to name a few. I wanted to help her allay her fears and so we had a chat about what we can do when we are scared. She recognised that when people are scared, they do the 'catch your breath, short sharp breathing pattern' and so we decided that a long deep breath might help. I then asked about what she is thinking when she's scared, take the dinosaur for example? Her answer was that it could hurt her. 'Instead of thinking that,' I said, 'can you think of a time when you feel safe and happy?' I melted inside with her reply, 'when I'm cuddling you, Daddy.' The next day we were in the swimming pool and I told her that I was going to throw her in the air so she can do a big splash. Realising this would mean going underwater, fear attempted the emotional hijack. 'Are you scared?' I asked. Immediately she smiled her knowing smile and took a deep breath. 'What are you thinking?' I said. 'Well, I don't need to think of you because you are already cuddling me.' Her defiance wins. Just to make sure she asked, 'you're not actually going to throw me, are you Daddy?' 'Of course not.' And what of Captain Hook? Well, she held my arm as he scowled his way through his most dastardly of monologues and as the pantomime boos and hisses subsided one voice could be heard across the auditorium, 'I'm not scared, he's actually quite funny, isn't he Daddy?' It received almost the biggest laugh of the show!

So, what about our physiology? We all know this! Describe how someone who is depressed would look physically. What are you thinking of? Looking down, hunched over, perhaps lying on a bed in a foetal position? You maybe had other images depending on your experience of depression, however, I would be surprised if any of you thought about skipping, laughing or dancing around a brightly decorated room with a party hat on blowing a whistle. Our breathing pattern perhaps has the most obvious effect on our physiology. I am sure we have all seen someone catch their breath following a shock and noticed how it can speed up when we get agitated. What is our response? 'Take a deep breath, relax'. Again, we all know this intuitively; it is being able to implement it through choice that is the difference. Since the first edition, I have done more research on breathing and breathing patterns. Breath control is an important aspect of mindfulness, yoga and many other useful exercises. It is key to preparation for an important event as well as regaining control in a high-pressure situation. However, in order to truly benefit from its use in the moments that you really need it, it is vital to have the emotional state control that will allow you the awareness in the moment to adapt your breathing in a way that benefits you. It is about recognising when you need to change something to get the results you wish for before your emotions have taken control in a negative way.

I was once coaching a very senior manager and it highlighted the need to understand and implement the whole rather than just dabbling with these techniques. A little bit of knowledge can be dangerous. His issue was public speaking, not uncommon, and it had become so much of a problem that he was consumed by the anxiety he created of meetings and presentations he had to attend or give. As these were weekly events they were always on his mind. His sleep was affected, his weekends disturbed and he was becoming noticeably short-tempered with his partner. (One to note for those who still think there is a difference between life and business coaching. There is not. Remember coaching is about getting the client into the most resourceful state they can be in order to make their own decisions not about telling them what to do.) It had got so bad that he was seriously considering quitting. To his credit he had recognised the importance of the issue for him and his family and after acknowledging his problem had sought help.

Unfortunately for my client the help he had sought in the past, had only allowed him to dabble. For instance, he had been told that his physiology had an effect on his emotional state but they had not linked it with his internal representation. So, while he stood tall and puffed out his chest in an effort to appear confident, his mind was playing him a complete mismatch. He had a constant internal dialogue the likes of: 'Who are you kidding?' 'This isn't you!' 'They can all tell you don't mean it'. None of which was helping and in fact for him personally he ended up feeling worse because of the intensity of the setback. This internal dialogue is not often in our conscious attention sufficiently enough to do something positive about it. What this means in reality is that our automatic responses are free to act on whatever movie our unconscious is playing in our mind. It is only when we interrupt this process and consciously decide on the internal representation we want that we are able to use it more resourcefully and have a positive effect on our own emotional state. Incidentally, my client is now able to speak in public without issue and he is more content with his home life too.

Have you noticed how quiet someone gets when they are lost? If in the car they will surely turn down the radio and ask everyone to stop talking. This is because their senses are becoming overloaded. When I was instructing army helicopter pilots in the art of navigation and map reading the very same would happen. The cockpit would become very quiet. The student now engrossed in their map and desperately trying to match it with the outside world below would slowly become less attentive to other events and miss radio calls, even unable to respond to simple questions from their instructor. Depending on their stage on the course this spiral decent, sometimes quite literally, would continue and on a battlefield this could be at best debilitating to the mission and at worst extremely dangerous. Only able to re-establish their position after taking a very important step: admitting that they are lost. Once the elephant in the room, or cockpit and that creates an interesting visual, is spoken aloud the relief is obvious and they can move on to execute the drills required to get back on track.

"We first need
    to acknowledge
        that we are lost
        in order to
        find our way to where
        we want to be"

How do we interrupt this process of automatic response? Well, you are now already a long way towards being able to do this because you have begun to increase your awareness of internal representation. You will steadily raise this awareness and notice what it is that you are thinking whilst experiencing your various emotional states. Remember not to judge the state you find yourself in, it is what it is, and setting up a conflict with yourself will not help. Better to be curious as to how you got there and how you will learn to decide on your emotional state in the future. When coaching it is often about asking the right question at the right time and self-application is no different. It is just that you need to be in a position of control even when in an unhelpful emotional state. This means that you need to recognise this state at its early stages before the dwelling and exaggeration sets in. Our tendency to exaggerate a scenario is what can deepen the process. I am convinced that over 90% of the things we worry about never actually happen. They are merely exaggerated and because of our powerful brains become seemingly real. Remember in evolutionary terms it is not that long ago that a human wandering around looking for the positives and oblivious to negatives would probably have been eaten; "Oh, my, what big teeth you have." We have a lot to overcome. Once you feel yourself developing an undesirable state, we will talk more about feelings in a minute, notice what you are playing in your mind and change it. Ask yourself questions like:

- What else could it mean?
- If I can change this belief, what will I be able to achieve?
- What if that image I'm imagining was made really small?
- Who was the last person I saw laugh?
- What would I need to know to achieve this task?

The questions you ask yourself will serve to re-focus your mind. They re-direct your attention. We know that our conscious attention can only handle about 4 pieces of information at any one time. Instead of allowing the unconscious to select these pieces, a well-timed and structured question gives us the ability to control our thoughts by choosing the information in our conscious attention.

Now remember that emotions and states are a mind-body experience. When you are in a certain state you feel it 'in your bones' as some would say. Don't just take my word for it though, remember for yourself. Has anything ever made you jump? How did you feel when scared? Exactly that, 'feel', maybe in the pit of your stomach. Have you ever seen a film of an audience 'watching' a scary movie? How they clutch themselves and each other. Afterwards the viewers will talk of how they could hardly breath or that it made them feel sick. These kinaesthetic sensations that we feel throughout our bodies are another powerful indicator of a state change. Various psychologists have debated throughout the years about which comes first the physical feeling or the mind's thoughts and therefore which causes the other. It would appear that as we are talking nanoseconds here, from an operator's point of view, i.e., from the point of view of each of us taking control of ourselves, it makes no discernible difference providing that we remember the mind-body interaction and the importance of affecting both. For some a change in our physiology is easier to detect first so it will help to raise the physical awareness of these kinaesthetic sensations too.

Our body alerts us as it is about to change state in a variety of ways. A lot of you will recognise how sensitive 'the pit of your stomach' is and how it can be a good indicator of change. I experienced a brilliant demonstration designed to increase this awareness by Carmen Bostic St Clair. It was during my NLP Trainer qualification. The course was conducted at quite a pace with plenty of tests requiring plenty of study. One afternoon, Carmen announced that we would be required to stay late that evening to repeat an area of study that she believed we were lacking in understanding. This would mean removing our preparation time for the next morning's test as well as affecting any other evening plans that one might have. Gradually the audience began to mutter as seated neighbours would share their discontent with the situation and how it was going to ruin their night and their chances of doing well in the coming morning's examination. To us all this was not fair, we have covered the importance of fairness amongst your staff as was demonstrated here, it is the one thing guaranteed to evoke emotion in almost all of us. With perfect timing, Carmen interrupted the mumbling. "Where do you feel it, right now? As you begin to get a little agitated and angry, your body is giving you a sensation, do you notice where it is?" It was a very clever piece of training, for most of us were indeed feeling the first signs of a state change. For me, I felt a hollow sensation in my stomach. I had become aware of my body's initial signal of a state shift and through this increased awareness I could use the warning to interrupt the pattern.

Another very useful exercise for controlling state is the use of 'Perceptual Positions'. This is a very simple way of looking at a situation from a different point of view. Take an argument as an example, it matters not what it is about. Instead of just stubbornly stating our case based on our own understanding, which the other person clearly does not share or else there would be no argument, look at the situation from their point of view, from the 2nd position (the 1st Position is as ourselves). Remembering that all actions have a positive intention, can you see why that person believes what they do? What would it be like to stand opposite yourself and argue the case? You may notice how aggressive you appear and therefore how defensive one could be against you. It may give you an insight into a mere misunderstanding that requires further explanation. You can take this even further to a 3rd position, as if you are an uninvolved observer taking in the scene of the argument. How do you think you come across then? It is why using a video recording of ourselves can be such a useful training tool to highlight traits we were unaware of. 'Perceptual Positions' is also a very good technique for diffusing an argument. If, after putting yourself in the other person's position, you can see their point of view then verbalising it before they are able to, can 'take the wind out of their sails' so to speak.

I was watching an English football match recently and observed as the referee 'booked' a player following a late challenge. The official went striding towards the player, waving his arms about and clearly shouting. He then reached into his pocket and brandished the yellow card right in the offender's face. Rather unsurprisingly the player in question responded defensively with equally aggressive gestures and a theatrical show of 'handbags' ensued. Later that day I watched the American Football Super Bowl and noticed how the officials merely stop the play and state the infringement to the crowd using a microphone. No confrontation with the players concerned and when they disagree the players are free to have their tantrum on the sideline.

We can learn to filter in order to focus. A leader is inundated with information from all angles and as with finding gold you often have to filter out a lot of crap. I believe you can train yourself to determine what is vital and what is not. Like anything it takes practice as well as learning to trust your instincts. Undoubtedly being in a calm state of mind, utilising what you have learnt in this chapter, will allow you to focus. Have you heard of people talk about when they are 'in the zone'? Often sports personalities describe a state when they felt like they were always one step ahead of everyone else. Watching them it can appear that they have all the time in the world compared to other players. It can be like this for anyone at the top of their game, including leaders. When your senses are tuned to your mind in such a way that they automatically filter what they are detecting and only allow through what is required in that moment. I have found the best combat pilots, the top sportsmen, the most effective presenters as well as the best leaders are those that are able to remain in control of their state when situations arise that could cause others to lose it.

This being 'in the zone' has become known in psychology as in a 'flow state' or simply 'in flow'. First introduced by the psychologist, Mihaly Csikszentmihalyi, and so-called because many of those he interviewed described their activity as simply flowing. The examples given above highlight that the situation of being 'in flow' is not necessarily a conscious choice. It is the result of many hours of practice and preparation that comes to fruition when engaged in a particular familiar activity. Indeed, bringing a conscious element to the occasion can be a blocker of flow. This is often witnessed in major sporting events when someone, seemingly cruising to victory, suddenly finds themselves making basic mistakes as they close in on the prize; think of a tennis player that has amassed a sizable lead over their opponent but is now double faulting on serve as the conscious mind begins to think about winning and they try to focus intentionally on something that has become almost natural. There are ways of bringing yourself back into flow, such as using triggers and even distraction; learned skills that I teach utilising NLP, hypnosis and other techniques, but what about choosing to go into flow in order to undertake a task or create transformational change? Well, whilst being able to access flow will not shortcut the time it takes to become an expert in your field, it can help you remain there, realise your potential or increase your performance in just about any activity you wish to undertake. Contrary to popular belief it appears that being in flow is not just for athletes, combat pilots and extreme sports, it is actually writers, computer programmers and others performing primarily cognitive functions that find themselves in a flow state. It is possible to access flow intentionally both individually and as a team through various triggers, again that I teach, as well as through transcranial magnetic stimulation, which I don't teach, although the research is fascinating. It is certainly an area requiring further study but who wouldn't benefit from being able to access a high-performance state at will? Incidentally, Csikszentmihalyi's research was about happiness and wellbeing; he noted that when one is in flow, due to the intense concentration of being in the zone, there is no capacity for thinking about anything else, not problems or what other people think. It stands to reason that if we could all find an activity,

THE LEADERSHIP SECRET

whatever it is, which gets us in a flow state, we would all benefit from the affect it has on us. Remember too that it is an individual experience based on your own challenge and skill level, so it is not necessary to be the best at any activity, it is necessary to be the best that you can be, in that moment.

One of the major benefits of a helicopter over a plane is its ability to land almost anywhere on an unprepared surface, not requiring a runway. One of the major difficulties when training military helicopter pilots for operations is the fact that a helicopter has the ability to land almost anywhere on an unprepared surface, not requiring a runway. Often that unprepared surface can be made up of loose material such as snow or sand that when confronted with the downwash of a helicopter's main-rotor, or two main-rotors in the case of the Chinook, will create a cloud that can bring the visibility down to literally inches. In Arctic conditions it is generally referred to as a whiteout and in the desert a brownout. The disorientation of such conditions has caught out many aviators with catastrophic consequences. It is certainly an occasion when the pilot needs to be in control of their emotional state, as the visual cues that they are used to depending on, are now useless. In Afghanistan the sand is so fine it is more comparable in form to talcum powder and so it was important that we developed a technique to assist the pilots as best we could. As part of the operational training team for the UK's Apache Attack Helicopter Fleet, I would experiment with other instructors as to the best options. The Apache is a pretty sophisticated piece of equipment but in brownout conditions it still requires the skill of the pilot to successfully get it on the ground in one piece and able to fly again. They do cost £36m each, approximately, not to mention the value of the crew, which is considerably more in my opinion!

One asset in the Apache is a radar altimeter that can accurately determine the height of the aircraft above the ground. Very useful in such circumstances. A separate radar system can also tell you your projected clearance above the ground in front of you. This will avoid the 'beep, beep, beep, bang!' situation that could occur. I've over dramatised there because it is quite possible that this is daylight and the aircrew are fully able to see that it is a clear area, only affected by the brownout conditions once in the latter stages of the approach when the downwash is able to lift the dust. Back in the cockpit, the pilot is able to set a designated height for

Learning Emotional State Control

the altitude warner that when passed through will alert the crew. The alert is in the form of a light, though not a very obvious one, and an audible warning of a digitally created voice that repeats "altitude low" every second or so. The warning, a female voice, will only cease when cancelled by one of the crew, by means of pushing a button, or when the aircraft lands, there being a switch within the undercarriage system.

My idea was to leave the cancelling of the voice warning to that switch on the undercarriage, the squat switch. What this means is that if one is set up on a controlled approach in a steady descent, then as the aircraft passes through the designated height, 10 feet for instance and remember by now you are already in brownout conditions, the warning "altitude low" will commence. In an ideal situation you may hear "altitude low, altitude low" before touching down and it automatically cancelling on the squat switch. It is worth pointing out that you will feel the touchdown! If you find yourself in a situation when you hear "altitude low, altitude low, altitude low, altitude low" it would mean that you have been between 10 feet and the ground for a few seconds. This means an increased risk of generating a lateral movement and therefore touching down with a sideways motion capable of tipping over the helicopter, a bad thing! I should have mentioned that if you climb above the designated height again it also cancels the warning. So, my planned procedure was: if you hear "altitude low" three times and you haven't touched down you must overshoot and attempt another approach.

I wanted to test that the warning would be sufficiently noticeable and so with a fellow instructor I set off to experiment, not in the desert to begin with I hasten to add. During the approach I asked my colleague to make as much noise and as many distractions as he could, which he willingly obliged, to see whether I could still pick up the warning. This wasn't just a case of shutting off certain senses, something we can do quite easily like the turning off the radio when we are looking for our final destination on a car journey. I had to be able to filter information in the auditory sense and react to the specific warning. I needed to remain calm and alert. This was testing a worst-case scenario for the pilots and it worked, and as far as I know the same technique is still used today.

As a Leader you are going to be put under pressure. Whether or not that pressure turns into stress is up to you. Yes really, it is up to you. I accept that many of you will still be skeptical regarding the amount of control we possess over our emotional state and perhaps still see this as automatic response but I can assure you this is a learned skill. Go to empoweredresiliencetraining.com to find out more.

You already have a number of tools to assist you in ensuring that you manage that pressure and alleviate stress. In his book, Better Under Pressure, Justin Menkes examines how it is that CEOs of some of the world's leading companies handle the pressure at the top, or don't in some circumstances. He concurs that people can learn to deal with pressure and advises his readers to get used to performing simple tasks in front of a critical audience under the added pressure of time. The experience is designed to help you learn that you can perform equally well in what some would term a stressful situation. I am a firm believer that with a positive attitude anyone can build their own resilience to pressure. As with most things in life that we wish to improve at, practice-practice-practice.

I was fortunate enough to be selected as the first Apache Attack Helicopter Display Pilot for the British Army Air Corps' display team the Blue Eagles. It was indeed a great honour to show the aircraft to the hordes of aviation enthusiasts across the country. As well as giving me the opportunity to speak face to face with various interested parties. It was important for me to portray the aircraft in its true role as a weapons' platform and so I enlisted the help of a pyrotechnics expert whose credits include a number of 'James Bond' films. Although it may have added to the potential complications, I wanted to make it obvious as to what the crews are doing day in, day out when on an operational tour. The flying would also be right on the edge of the allowable flight envelope to demonstrate its impressive capability. In choreographing such a display I sought the advice of a number of experienced instructors as well as test pilots and a demonstration pilot from the USA. Armed with their information I set about tying together as many manoeuvres in the best possible sequence in order to show the incredible machine from as many angles and as close to the crowd-line as the regulations would allow.

Recruiting non-aviators as well as fellow pilots to watch a few practices, I sought to find out what looked good from the point of view of a spectator. Generally, those on the ground have no idea how difficult a particular manoeuvre is and are equally impressed by a simple lateral crowd pass as they are loop the loop. I will leave the details about the actual flying to my aviation memoirs as this is about 'emotional state control' and in this case, as with any performance-based event, the preparation was key. Once the routine had been finalised, I set about committing it too memory. Having written it this was a fairly easy task that I accomplished by visualising the complete routine and running it over and over in my mind. There were certain parameters that were set as limitations for a display. These included weather limitations such as wind and minimum cloud base. Hitting such limits would mean cancelling the flight or a change in the display, for example only including the low-level elements to account for a low cloud ceiling, as was the case at RAF Leuchars near Edinburgh, when the weather was so bad we were the only ones to conduct a display. The Typhoon did manage a take-off but went straight into cloud and so conducted a radar approach back to the airfield.

Before each individual display, I would confirm I had all necessary information such as radio frequencies, crowd line markers, holding points, timings, etc. and then I would visualise and walk-through the routine taking into account the day's wind direction. This would be done at the last possible moment before climbing aboard. Once strapped in, my co-pilot, Tommo, would confirm any points we'd made in the pre-flight brief and when airborne he would run through a few last minutes confirmation checks from a list we had made as things had cropped up during training. Ensure the monocle sight is securely fastened to the helmet being one as the added g-force had removed it on one practice! The routine we developed assisted in making the whole experience appear familiar and expected even under new circumstances. This familiarity helped me remain calm and focused on the job in hand and not on the 100, 000 or so pairs of eyes watching me. Remaining in control of my state also allowed me to react to the unexpected as happened when in the holding pattern just seconds away from our first display. The warning panel suddenly lit up along with the audible warning, 'the APU is on fire'. Not really what you want to hear at any time, let alone just before your debut show. I instinctively descended the aircraft into the closest available field as Tommo carried out the necessary drills to fire the extinguishers. The emergency had jumped in order of priority ahead of the intended routine and our calm state of mind had allowed our attention to be diverted.

Have you seen the film, 'An Officer and a Gentleman'? It stars, Richard Gere as a US Navy Officer under training who just wants to complete the course and 'fly jets'. One of the many hurdles in the way is

THE LEADERSHIP SECRET

the dreaded 'crash over water' simulator. Lisa Eilbacher plays the very nervous, Casey Seeger, a fellow candidate, who is seen hesitating at the start position of the simulator, where the mock cockpit is raised up a steep slope ready to be released and hurled back down into the pool before allowing the 'would be' pilot to escape from their inverted, underwater position. Any candidate refusing to complete the task is forced to DOR, Drop On Request, and is off the course. The helicopter world has its own version and for the British military the Underwater Escape Training Unit at RNAS Yeovilton houses precisely that version, a piece of equipment affectionately known as 'The Dunker'. Actually, it houses more than one dunker as each one represents a specific type of aircraft, a mockup of the inside, used to simulate a helicopter ditching into water.

The training is indeed one of the legendary hurdles that all military aircrew must overcome to gain their wings. It doesn't stop there, as the training is part of a currency requirement that must take place at least every two years throughout one's career. Raised above the water with its passengers and crew all strapped in, the capsule is then dropped into the water and after all motion has stopped the escape begins. The different runs gradually get more and more tricky for the escapees as various exits are blocked, the capsule is also inverted and the lights are extinguished. In the latter dunks you are required to use the STASS (Short Term Air Supply System) before escaping. The STASS is a miniature bottle of compressed air designed to give you a limited number of breaths in order to accomplish an escape, should you be winded in the crash. It may sound like an easier escape but in reality, it just increases the time before you break the surface. For those of you used to scuba diving, the regulator on the STASS requires a suck closer to a Dyson than that of a normal breath. Even as a pretty strong swimmer, I was a lifeguard before joining the Army, it can be quite an unpleasant situation; waiting upside down harnessed into your seat, awaiting a tap on the head from the training staff, the indication to use your STASS.

It is a prime example of the virtues of emotional state control. Those that have problems exiting the module have allowed the emotional hijack to happen. Their internal representation is totally consumed by images of being trapped and drowning. These thoughts take up the required focus to execute a controlled exit, there is literally no more space in their conscious attention to remember the drills and they end up getting snagged or unable to release the buckle. It is an unnatural experience, upside down and underwater, in the dark and with limited breath. On the few occasions when either my STASS had malfunctioned or my exit was blocked, I would only ever be thinking positively and I would be forcing my mind to do so. 'I'm okay, I know the drills, I will get out, I can do this and I am calm'. This positive mindset allowed me to get to the surface whereas thinking, 'I am stuck, I am doomed, I will drown and there is no way out,' obviously has a negative effect on the escape. And what of 'Seeger'? She decides she can do it, agrees to the release, hurtles down the slide, is inverted and submerged. She frees herself and climbs out of the pool realising the things she was worrying about never actually happened and asks, 'can I go again?'

"Calm is not always the answer, it is about Controlling Emotion, not Eradicating it."

On a fairly routine flight in Bosnia, it's always the routine ones you have to watch, we lost power to one of our two engines and I, along with my fellow pilot, were too calm for the situation we were in and that could have made it far worse. I was attached to the Royal Navy's Commando Helicopter Force flying the Sea King helicopter and our role for NATO was the Immediate Response Team. A United States Marine Corps Major, also on attachment to the Royal Navy and also named Chris, captained our aircraft that day. I was the co-pilot and in the cabin was our aircrewman, Higgie, a Royal Marine, and Jo, a Royal Air Force nurse. A truly joint effort. On the way to the field hospital, we were tasked with a drop-off at a communication station sat perched on the highest peak within our area. The Viterog is over 6000' above sea level and a lot further than that from civilisation. The dedicated soldiers manning the various radios spent most of their tour completely cut off due to the weather and the thousands of mines surrounding the solitary building, often reliant on the heli-borne replenishment.

Our cargo today, though not supplies, was arguably more welcome. The bulging mailbag containing various morale boosts in the form of messages and gifts from home. Messages that could very easily have been lost forever. Chris has a voice to rival the singer, Barry White.

THE LEADERSHIP SECRET

Having listened to his deep gravel over the phone, I was surprised to find it emanate from such a small stature, when we met. In the time we served together, I think I saw him lose his temper on maybe three occasions, and all three due to the Flight Commander, they did not get on. At all other times he was as laid back as a surfer doing the limbo. On this flight he was hands-on the controls whilst I handled the communications and monitored the flight systems. Being at altitude, where the air is thin, we would expect to need most of the power available from the two Rolls Royce Gnome engines, to execute a safe landing. Unfortunately, one of them would let us down.

On short finals to the landing pad, a cleared area of concrete barely large enough to fit the three wheels of our undercarriage, Chris was smoothly controlling the approach. Our eyes in the back, Higgie, confirmed our projected flight path was clear whilst Jo sat in the open cabin doorway enjoying the view and the moment to relax before her upcoming duty that could see her attending to any possible injury and incident.

A sudden change in tone from the engine alerted me to an impending problem. Not quite over the landing pad, the aircraft dropped, the sinking motion catching my breath. Luckily for us the left wheel had caught the concrete but the right had slipped off and the tailwheel had no chance. In the front it was quite matter-of-fact as the drills kicked in. "The Left engine's unlatched, it needs manual advance," I stated as I reached for the manual control lever, "confirm?" I checked with the aircraft Captain. "Yeah, sure," came the reply as he did his best to stop the King from sliding off the edge. The intercom erupted with a series of desperate commands to 'lift up' and general expletives from the rear cabin. Higgie, was understandably concerned. The Sea King is over 50' long and when pivoting on the front wheels this means a relatively huge drop in height at the cabin door. Added to the situation, Jo had fallen out as we hit the ground, dangling on her harness until Higgie had reached out and pulled her back in. "Hold on, mate, we're on one engine," I was still perhaps understating the implications as I advanced the manual control lever, urging it to take charge of the malingering engine. Thankfully it did, and Chris's steady hands lifted us properly over the spot and we touched down safely.

I should have been a lot more vocal at the onset of the emergency, ensuring that the whole crew heard. Our aircrewman was doing his job in alerting us of a problem that he was unaware we already knew about. This extra noise over the intercom could have blocked vital correspondence between Chris and I had we not already come to a conclusion of the problem and carried out the immediate actions required to overcome it. Sometimes you may need to appear excited for the benefit of others, even when calm within.

Let us summarise Emotional State Control. If we wish to control something it is a good place to start with what it is we wish to control. Understanding that emotional state is a product of both Physiology and Internal Representation highlights the areas that we are able to affect a change. An increase in our own State Awareness is crucial to enabling that change to be made. We are able to raise this awareness of our state by consciously noticing our own physiology including our posture and breathing pattern. And we are able to notice what is being played out in our mind. Asking ourselves questions enables us to redirect the focus of the mind. Knowing what we now know we are able to alter an unresourceful state and choose to access a desired emotional state.

As we develop our own skills to assist us with making the right decisions, it is important that we remember the importance of the development of those under our charge. It is a significant difference between those who merely manage their staff and those who lead them. In the next chapter we will look at effective training and its implementation.

Thankfully, I did see Terry again, he would go on to make a full recovery. A great deal of leadership issues were encountered following the incident. With my team we set about searching whether any lessons could be learned for future operations. As it turned out we came to the conclusion that our standard operating procedures, which included the wearing of a helmet whilst driving, could well have saved his life and despite my frustrations at the time, the procedure for activating the IRT was also pretty robust. What I also sought, though indirectly through my second in command, was feedback on how I had performed in the situation. A combination of my desire to improve and the working relationship with my 'number two' that allowed such open and frank discussions was paramount to my development, although I don't think I fully recognised this fact at the time. My Staff Sergeant was a very experienced soldier who had served with airborne, commando and

THE LEADERSHIP SECRET

airmobile brigades and yet I don't think he had encountered a boss so keen for honest feedback. The feedback he gave me was that those present were impressed at how involved I had become in ensuring that everything possible was being done and that it was clear how much I cared. From his point of view, I had come across as 'a little bit too excited!' That was the moment when I learned to control my emotions.

> *"The mind is its own place,*
> *and in itself can make*
> *a heaven of hell,*
> *a hell of heaven…"*
>
> John Milton, 'Paradise Lost'

Learning Emotional State Control

Points to Remember - Emotional State Control:

- I make my best decisions when I am calm and in control.

- Our Emotional State is the result of our internal representation and our physiology.

- How we perceive a situation can determine our state, everything is relative.

- Emotional Intelligence is about raising awareness of emotion and how to use it.

- My mind is still 'Me', and it acts with a positive intention.

- I can avoid internal conflict by accepting 'it is what it is' without judging.

- We can interrupt previous automatic patterns when we learn the signals and redirect out focus with questions.

- I may be put under pressure; it is up to me whether this causes stress.

- I can choose my emotional state.

- I am able to question my own thoughts in order to switch focus.

6

DEVELOPING YOUR TEAM

*"Train for Everything;
and more Importantly,
Train for Anything"*

As a Leader it is incumbent upon you to develop your team. This is a key role that sets Leaders aside from mere managers. I took great pleasure from witnessing the progression those under my command achieved. Their success was my success and vice versa. There are some in positions of authority that almost resent the success of those in their employment and see everyone as a potential threat. This is most unfortunate because if you are not getting the best from your team then as a team you are not performing to your best and that ultimately means you are not leading. I delighted in the fact that the longer I was in a job the more the staff could do, eventually performing tasks that they would have been unable to when I arrived. Apart from anything else it then allowed me more time to look at how we could move forward and become even better.

"Qui Docet Discit"

An imperative to the development of a team is relevant, realistic training. Far too many heads of business take no interest in the actual training of their staff. Seemingly content to leave it to the HR department and then complaining when the finished article is not to their liking. If you get the training right then every single member of your staff will meet your basic requirement.

The secret to effective training is allowing those involved to get it wrong. Actually explaining that it is okay to make mistakes. When conducting the operational command and tactics training for the British Army Air Corps' frontline helicopter crews, I would begin with an honest admission. I expected and welcomed mistakes. This was the place to find our weaknesses and to do something about them. All I asked was that decisions were made; apathy was not an option. If you make a decision and it doesn't work out, you can analyse and revise. By seeing the outcomes of not necessarily the best decision it is easier to learn the 'whys and wherefores'. We developed a culture of honesty. An openness to being able to admit where someone was unsure about something or were certain they had done something wrong.

Incidentally, this common practice in aviation is a must for safety. The consequences of someone not being able to admit to a mistake for fear of severe punishment could see unserviceable aircraft take to the skies. Perhaps the global financial crisis could have been averted if some of the major banks had adopted such a policy. Apparently, junior workers were not only unable to question their bosses' actions but would rarely admit to a mistake, for like others before them they could lose their job. This meant that instead of catching a problem at an early stage, an issue would be hidden whilst it magnified into even more damaging proportion.

Of course, a culture of honesty is a lot easier to implement with the ability to replay events using video and audio systems able to see into the cockpit but nevertheless it changed attitudes. It is important that training is informative and not merely testing. Once there has been instruction then of course put it to the test. The cycle of such training would usually begin with my staff pointing out a plethora of mistakes during the early missions, most of which the crews would be unaware. After further instruction this would develop to the crews themselves highlighting areas for improvement through their own increased awareness and in time there wouldn't be any mistakes, well no major ones anyway.

Throughout the training the focus was always on what it was for. Preparing to go to a war zone should focus the mind of course but it was more than that. I had been to that war zone as had my staff and we knew what mattered and perhaps more importantly what did not and we were committed to deliver the best preparation available for our colleagues. I used to state at the start of training when it would appear that I was forever highlighting issues that I only do this because I care. I had a positive intention of conducting the best training I could and if I didn't do that then I would not be being professional. "Worry when I stop pointing out where you can improve, not when I do."

A proud moment for me and one that I remember as a moment that justified the work, was when a young Captain, having recently returned from an operational tour, made a point of finding me whilst visiting the Corps HQ. The point he wanted to make was that when all hell was going on around him and he found himself in a position where his decisions would be the difference, his first thought was that this was precisely what he'd been taught in training.

In the first edition, I outlined the learning cycle and the stage we go through as we learn a new skill:
- Unconscious Incompetence
- Conscious Incompetence
- Conscious Competence
- Unconscious Competence

Let us examine the cycle with a skill such as driving a car. Firstly, there is 'Unconscious Incompetence': When we are children, although we know what a car is, we are unaware of what it takes to drive one as well as being unable to. 'Conscious Incompetence' is when we begin to learn to drive. We now know what it takes to drive to a set standard but as yet are unable to achieve this standard. At the 'Conscious Competence' stage, we manage to achieve the desired standard when we give it our conscious attention. Finally, we arrive at 'Unconscious Competence' and in terms of the driving analogy this is where we drive without having to concentrate too much or being aware of the skill. Have you ever driven a familiar route and having arrived could not remember any of the journey? There will be occasions when we revert back to the 'Conscious Competence' with regards to driving, perhaps in poor weather conditions and on unfamiliar roads when the extra concentration is again required.

All of what I described above remains valid, and let us re-examine the cycle with what we now know about 'flow' from the previous chapter. I am sure you can recognise the stage of 'Unconscious Competence' could also be described as being in the zone or being in flow. We are not consciously thinking about the task in hand, we are performing as if on auto-pilot, our mind and actions in harmony 'flowing' in the moment. The most exciting aspect is that we can, with practice, make a conscious decision and action to enter a flow state. When I would conduct a walk-through rehearsal before each flying display and follow a set routine as I took to the sky, although I may not have been aware of it at the time, I was using anchors, triggers, visualisation, and breathing patterns to ensure I accessed my flow state. Have you noticed how some Formula 1 drivers conduct reaction exercises and follow familiar rituals with their engineers before they climb into their car? Although it takes training, it is possible to make a choice to get in the zone, which does not mean that flow will not still come in its naturally occurring form. But being able to deliberately access flow brings more possibility to high performance and a new stage to the cycle, 'Conscious Unconscious Competence'. We now have:

- Unconscious Incompetence
- Conscious Incompetence
- Conscious Competence
- Unconscious Competence (Flow)
- Conscious Unconscious Competence (Deliberate access to flow)

Understanding this cycle of learning helps us to ensure efficient training programmes are developed for our staff. They must include raising the awareness of a new skill through showing them how to develop the skill. Moving on to practising the new skill and finally becoming so familiar with the skill that they are able to take on other tasks simultaneously. An example would be learning a particular presentation format required of a business. At first unaware of the format, a new team member is taught the format and allowed the time to develop and practice, the format eventually becoming so proficient that they are able to use it at a moment's notice. To ensure peak performance throughout a presentation, that team member can be taught how to deliberately access flow.

It is a good idea to make the training as realistic as possible. Part of my mission when deployed to Afghanistan was to find out ways where we could do exactly that. On one of my first missions, I had a perfect example to take back. I was flying in the rear seat piloting the Apache for the Squadron's Operations Officer, Dave, a Royal Navy Officer on an exchange with the Army. I had known Dave for many years going back to when I had been the exchange officer with the Royal Navy. He is a very calm, controlled man and I always enjoyed working with him. We had been tasked to an area where soldiers had come under fire and we were to provide covering fire allowing them to extract from the situation. Best speed was required to get there as quickly as possible. As I raised the collective lever, increasing the power and accelerating our helicopter to full speed I noticed an unusual vibration run throughout the fuselage. Flying helicopters, you get used to the various shakes and sounds they can produce but this felt very alien to me. Not to Dave though, it felt just as it always did. To me it was as if the aircraft was struggling. After a brief discussion and a bit of experience searching in my mind it was clear that as the aircraft was operating at a high all-up-mass, i.e., it was heavy, and the conditions were hot, it was merely that this was how an Apache felt on the limits. A feeling that we just didn't encounter in the temperate conditions of the UK, and before then had no need to replicate whilst training in the USA. We added such a sortie to our next round of training to ensure pilots were used to the differences before arriving on such a tour.

Why is it so important to make the training as realistic as possible? Our response or reaction to any given situation is based on our own individual life experiences stored in the 'internal library' we discussed in the chapter 'Learning Emotional State Control'. This vast library has been created throughout our life influenced by our experiences and what we have been taught by our parents, teachers, figures in authority and just about everyone we have ever seen and everything we have ever done. These combined experiences have had a greater or lesser effect in shaping our beliefs and our understanding of what we hold true. So these beliefs are also stored in the library and used as a reference point when an internal representation is formed.

Given a completely new situation as a child with no form of reference to relate to we react accordingly, perhaps with curiosity and humour as we see a little dark, spindly legged object run across the floor. After witnessing an adult's fear at the harmless spider, we now possess a frame of reference with which to compare in the future. In this instance, if all the child ever witnesses is fear around the spider, the chances are that the child will adopt that fear too. The more experiences we have in life the richer our resources become in handling different situations. It is up to us to recognise the importance of our internal library and to ensure it offers choice and flexibility. When a belief instilled in us only offers one choice of response, guess what? That is what you get every time. That is of course what a phobic response is. By making the training as close to the real thing as possible it provides a familiar frame of reference within our mind, allowing a choice when responding.

Now, although I have laboured the point of making training as realistic as possible, there is going to be a limit and at some point you can switch to 'training for anything'. I see many a company that gets bogged down with trying to ensure that every possible permutation is covered by an extensive and detailed programme. Inevitably such a programme is then the first to be cut when money is an issue, and when is money not an issue? Surely it is more beneficial to develop the minds of your staff. I would much rather have a team able to think on their feet and deal with any given situation. 'No plan survives initial contact with the enemy'. It is a common phrase and so true. A business cannot be run solely on checklists. Businesses, successful ones, are run by people, and more importantly people able to make decisions and adapt to a changing environment. Flexible minds able to remain calm and controlled, allowing best possible outcomes. In that light then, how do you make the training realistic for an unexpected situation?

Unexpected situations require flexibility of thought and an ability to remain calm when something happens that is, well, unexpected! (Which is why Learning Emotional State Control is so important). There you have it, then. Provide training that is designed to develop the mind and body as one. Set up situations that require your staff to think on their feet, to respond to a totally new circumstance. This does not mean that you need to provide life/death situations or you need them all to swing across an imaginary river with just a Sainsbury's carrier bag and a piece of hairy string. There is a place for command tasks and it is not necessarily here. It could be as simple as how to handle the fact that a new customer wants to double your current productivity. I have often found it a useful development exercise to tackle problems from a totally different viewpoint. In setting a task, ask how various groups might approach the situation. How would a football team, an astronaut, a scientist, teachers, kids or artists solve the problem? The goal is to develop lateral thinking and creative minds are welcome.

Some seem to hold the view that one has either a business brain or a creative brain. We are all capable of both. As a child we played within a make-believe frame as free as we could imagine. Lego mixed with Action Man and the Teletubbies had tea with Barbie without rules. As we aged so did the influence of others to restrict our creative side within certain boundaries. It is up to us to allow this side to again be free to express itself without restrictions. The balance, in terms of how these ideas are implemented, can be restored once the ideas have been heard. My colleague and I ran an exercise with a mobile phone company using the 'different viewpoint' approach and it resulted in a totally new concept for how they offered their insurance to customers, a concept that if it had been brought up during the department's weekly meeting would have surely been rejected immediately. Remember to provide the outcome you desire and to make clear the positive intention behind the training. You are aiming to develop thought patterns and an ability to deal with new situations. You are now training for anything. You are building resilience in your staff that will enable them to handle the pressure of the unknown.

One particular training discipline that as aircrew I had the fortune to be subjected to was Resistance to Interrogation training. I say fortune because it provided me with a number of experiences that allowed me do develop certain resourceful states that have come in useful since. Resistance to Interrogation training came in conjunction with Escape and Evasion training. Obviously if the latter did not work the chances are you would need the former. The training has come a long way since I first experienced it when it was conducted with little instruction and was almost seen as just an unpleasant test that one had to go through to fly for a living. The rules at the time meant that we were extremely limited in how we should act in the Conduct after Capture scenario. A lot of it made little sense as those we were likely to come up against at that time as now were certainly not likely to have heard of the Geneva Convention let alone signed it.

The training was designed to come after a period of escape and evasion whereby all those taking part were already sleep deprived and had eaten very little for a number of days. This was to add to the demands on the body and mind. An untrained mind can begin to play some pretty intense tricks after prolonged sleep deprivation. Combined with the strip searches, ill-fitting clothing, a blindfold and damp, cold conditions were the various sessions of interrogation and time spent in a stress position. A

Developing Your Team

stress position was where one had to remain in a given position, such as squatting down with arms stretched out, for an unknown length of time. Any deviation from the position would invite a 'polite' reminder from the unseen captors. For me, however, the training seemed to work almost in reverse. I was in a lot of pain during the stress positions, mainly due to an injury I had been given when 'captured', and so the interrogation sessions came as an almost relief. 'Almost' relief, they weren't that pleasant either but I did find it fascinating viewing the various tactics employed. Even though at no point did I think it was real, and others did by the way, it gave me the knowledge that should the unthinkable happen I would at least have some form of reference to base my response and reactions on. The training worked in a variety of ways: It was unlike any other experience we had encountered and therefore gave us a new perspective and outlook. At times it was indeed challenging and in completing the course one experienced a sense of achievement and gave us a number of resources on which to draw in the future. Perhaps most of all, due to the collective experience, it served to deepen the team dynamic as difficult situations that 'we go through together' seem to do very well.

A sure way for a Leader to develop their team is to develop their own coaching skills. Have you ever noticed the difference between being told an answer and being given the tools to find out the answer for yourself? We get a sense of achievement when we do something for ourselves, when we solve the problem. This sense of achievement also assists the learning process by improving understanding and generally making it easier to recall in the future, as it has been a multi-sensory experience. Have you witnessed someone doing a crossword when they verbalise the clues and then when someone says the answer straight away, they are annoyed? How many times have you been trying to think of something and when someone says that they know the answer you have stated, "don't tell me, I know this?" Why do we say that? Someone has the answer and is willing to give it to us and yet we want to come up with it ourselves. Even the simple act of remembering gives us the satisfaction of accomplishment. It is why there are so many quizzes in the world. The same is true for physical exercises too: We can buy cakes but we like to bake, fly up mountains but we like to climb, hire a decorator but we like to 'do it yourself'. The end result is the same and yet different: we have a cake, we are on a mountain, and we have a newly painted room. It is the journey, of course, that makes the incredible difference, and it is the journey experience that gives that sense of achievement and adds to our personal development.

Are you providing a journey for your staff? When coaching a team, we can use Socratic questions to develop staff. The right question can be used to focus attention in the required area. That is what questions do, they re-focus our attention. A Leader is able to use questions to develop their team as well as inspire. 'How can we turn this experience into a positive?' 'What lessons can we learn from this situation?' 'What is important to you about the work you do?'

> *"Where there's a will there's a way,*
> *Where there's a way there's a will."*

Technological advancement has enabled training to become a lot more immersive with the use of synthetic systems such as Visual Reality. Equally as important is the ability record data and playback to those under training during an after-action review. A more in-depth understanding of the learning experience is possible through biometric data capture, real time playback and more structured assessment process. The world of behavioural science allows for more efficient and effective training in almost all situations. Accepting that one needs a certain amount of drive to learn new skills, the will; when those under training are able to see tangible results demonstrating progression, this has a positive effect on inspiration. A word of warning, there are a lot of organisations with some pretty lofty claims about the use of technology so be sure to do your research. It is becoming very easy to capture data but it is still a scarce commodity to find a training team using that data to good effect or providing an effective intervention for change. Another word of warning, who are you getting to decide on or conduct your training? I have seen many organisations leave the training to the HR (human resources) department with little or no input from the leadership team. There are many in HR that have only ever been in HR. They are not, necessarily best placed to determine the training and development of the business. Staff training is the future of the business, think carefully about whom you want with the responsibility for that training.

Developing Your Team

If your team is engaged in a particular role that you used to do yourself then there may be the need on occasion for you to act more as a mentor. It may even be the case that within your team some members will be called upon to mentor others. Remember this still does not mean that you are telling them precisely what to do; it is merely a process that allows you to impart your own experience. A friend of mine, Leon Taylor, an Olympic 10-metre platform synchronised diving Silver Medalist and the creator of (at the time) the world's most difficult dive, explains the role of mentoring in some detail in his book 'Mentor-The Most Important Role You Were Never Trained For'. Based on his experiences mentoring, Tom Daley, the 2009 10-metre platform diving world champion, he highlights some useful tips for such a specific role.

In the next chapter, we will look at some more practical application. Highlighting tried and tested techniques that will allow you to get the very best from your team. As with all advice, don't just take my word for it, I invite you to experience it for yourself. It is only by our own curiosity and willingness to experiment that we find the right solutions for ourselves.

"I have always found that plans are useless, but planning is indispensable"
DD Eisenhower

THE LEADERSHIP SECRET

Points to Remember – Developing Your Team:

- Train for Everything; and more importantly Train for Anything.

- The development of the team is a crucial role for a Leader.

- Qui Docet Discit: He, who teaches, learns.

- Mistakes when training are a learning opportunity.

- Split training between realistic and surprising.

- Developing coaching skills can assist with staff development.

7

UTILISING MISSION TRUST

"Explain What is required and Why,
rather than How,
and be amazed by
the Creativity"

I have been asked on many occasions how to get the most from a team and the simple answer is to trust them. 'Mission Trust' is an adaptation of a process used in the British Army whereby a commander will tell their subordinates what they want to achieve and why without necessarily going into how. It works equally well in the corporate world and my findings thus far, as they were in the army, is that when people are given the responsibility and latitude to be creative the results can be truly amazing. Many have in-built limitations seeded through years of both society as a whole and their own personal view of what 'someone like them' should be able to achieve and when you give them the freedom and support to experiment with their own ideas, they themselves can be surprised by their own creation. These limiting beliefs can be removed and as a Leader you have an important role in doing so.

Many bosses have the misguided view that their role is to continually tell people what to do, constantly looking over the shoulder and using the 'long screwdriver'. You may have worked for some of these. This strict command and control outlook, that a great deal of people tend to associate with the military, only has a place on the drill square. A much looser approach that allows freedom to manoeuvre is the norm elsewhere and especially on the battlefield. It is this flexibility and openness to

Mission Trust that so many corporations are crying out for in this modern era. In my time in the army this approach came naturally as its foundation lies in the mutual trust that had been developed throughout the team. Once a team is being led then they will begin to work for each other.

The motto of the Royal Military Academy Sandhurst is 'Serve to Lead' and those three words give a true indication of what is required in order to make this work. Do you appreciate the role of a Leader as actually serving those you lead? They are your responsibility. When mutual trust is present then as a Leader you are able to set the course for the shared objective and allow your team members to take their own journey. Understanding where they need to get to and why enables them to make immediate decisions about obstacles in the way in order to remain on track. That is the difference that makes the difference, the empowerment to make decisions in this world of 'want an answer now'. This does not detract from your role as the Leader as their increased understanding of the mission allows them to recognise game changing situations that do require your input. This process is a key enabler to running multiple projects. Remember, Leaders are very self-aware and in this situation they 'know what they don't know' and are therefore able glean from their staff the missing pieces of the puzzle. The Leader is still required to put the pieces together.

When you lead a team of specialists this becomes even more apparent. I have been very fortunate in my career to have in my team some extremely talented and knowledgeable personnel, all experts in their field. In becoming these experts, they spent years studying and operating within their specialised trade. I depended on their knowledge and trusted the information given to me was accurate and valid. Now, I wasn't completely ignorant to their skill-set as I made a point of finding out as much as I could to assist with my own decision making, nevertheless the team as a whole and me as the Leader relied on certain individuals in order to complete our mission. This is not an unlikely scenario in many jobs and it requires no small amount of humility to get the best out of any specialist.

The intention in terms of Mission Trust is to give enough information about the overall desired outcome to allow your staff to work with the freedom mentioned above without over complicating the situation. Along with knowing your intention it is worth outlining your line manager's intention too and perhaps their line manager as well, should they have one. This really helps to build a picture as to where everyone fits in. With these outlines it is advisable to talk in terms of the effect one wishes to achieve without being too specific. For example, it may be sufficient to state that the intention is to expand the business's customer base without going into the various strategic ideas for doing so at this level.

> *"The day soldiers stop bringing you their problems is the day you have stopped leading them. They have either lost confidence that you can help them or concluded that you do not care. Either case is a failure of leadership."*
>
> Colin Powell

When working in terms of 'effects required' it allows creativity within the workforce to discover ways to create such an effect. A clear definition of what is meant by a certain effect in terms of outcome may be required in order to recognise when the desired outcome is achieved. This can be in the form of specific success criteria. These definitions will often only need to be determined once and as a company gains experience working with an 'effects-based process' innovation, in the form of ways to create the effects, will flow. Remember the leader does not always have to come up with the best idea, they are there to recognise the best idea and to drive it forward.

When I was working in West Africa it would have been a poor use of my time to deal with the constant changes and countless variables that one encounters in a developing country. I had fully briefed my assistant on what I was there to achieve and why, and so whilst I conducted the various meetings and negotiations he could get on with the logistics. Understanding the overall outcome requirement, he was able to deal with the unserviceable helicopters, overflowing rivers, unhelpful border officials and demanding Chiefs with minimal involvement from me. When people are given the responsibility and latitude to be creative the results may surprise you, in a positive way. Many of the limitations have been seeded through years of both society as a whole and their own personal view of what they should be able to achieve and when you give them the freedom and support to experiment with their own ideas, they themselves can be surprised by their own creation. As I have said this approach to a work environment can take some time because right across hierarchal structure the trust and focus needs to be mutually present.

Using the skills you learnt in the chapter 'Getting to Know Your Staff' you can begin building a trusting working environment and it is often a good place to start with where everyone fits in, what their role is and why it is important to the business as a whole. I am reminded of a presentation I attended recently from a senior executive of the toy manufacturer Lego. As one might expect from a toy making company the presentation was both fun and light-hearted and more importantly delivered a valuable message to those present. For the speaker ran through exactly how Lego goes about initiating new staff and that all new staff no matter what level they enter the company are treated to an induction. This includes a presentation on the history of Lego, the aims of the company as a whole, where that individual fits into the business and what the work they will be doing means to the overall outcome. She emphasised from the start that the company was a family owned and run business and that all of the staff were welcomed into the family-oriented atmosphere and shown how they are valued from day one. There have been many psychological studies on what it is that people look for in a work environment and something that provides satisfaction and a sense of belonging coupled with a sense of worth is very high up the list. It would appear that as a species we humans feel comfortable when we feel that we are a valued member of the team, we are after all pack-animals at heart.

- Do your staff know about the company?
- Do they understand their role within it?
- Do they feel a valued member of the team?

It is extremely common these days for new employees to be shown a long list of their job responsibilities as a checklist by which their overall annual grade will be determined and it is far too easy for this to be done in a somewhat clinical manner with a total avoidance of any personal touch. Although there are potential legal reasons that require such a list to exist and for official acknowledgement one can ensure that such matters are carried out 'as well as' a suitable induction and face-to-face discussion rather than 'instead of'. It is likely that a new member of staff may feel some initial nervousness about meeting their new boss especially as with many companies, an HR department may do prior interviews and of course first impressions count both ways. The impression you give as a Leader in the first meeting could well determine how effective that person will be for you. As I have alluded to before, it is a perfect opportunity to find out information about someone that a human resources or personnel recruitment agency may not have thought necessary to ask for they are not the ones who want to know what makes someone tick and therefore what can be used to inspire and assist with personal development.

The frontline operational training that I was a major part of developing was not confined to the aircrew. The Apache helicopter was so new in service that every member of a regiment needed to learn the additional skills it required of them to maintain its operational effectiveness. The maintenance crews of the Royal Electrical Mechanical Engineers (REME) were getting to grips with a completely new type of aircraft. The big and robust airframe housing a digital network of computers had brought with it a whole new experience from the analogue machines we were used to flying. The increased logistical footprint on the battlefield had the statisticians busy calculating various formulas for keeping it running. And for the groundcrew came the additional responsibility of establishing arming and re-fueling teams crucial to the success of a mission. A good friend and a huge personality within the Army Air Corps conducted the ground training. Rab, a larger than life, Scot, had been promoted through the ranks to Regimental Sergeant Major before being awarded a commission. Now a fellow Major we would work closely together in order to coordinate the ground and air training. He worked tirelessly to ensure his troops were best prepared for the situations they would eventually find themselves in. At the start of every course, I would speak to the groundcrew. I would explain what an important role they had in the operation of the Apache. Their work would have a direct input into the success of future missions. How well they worked as a team when maintaining the rocket pods and how quickly they managed to turn around an aircraft involved in a fire support task meant that lives depended on them. They weren't required to work at the pace of a Formula 1 pit-stop crew but they did require the same level of professionalism. There could be many reasons for a rocket failing to fire, most of them would be out of their control, but every time one fired correctly it was a testament to their good work. They knew their role; they knew the role of the aircraft and they knew the part their team played within the whole mission.

Have you heard about the 'First Follower'? Derek Sivers gave an interesting talk on TED about 'How to start a movement'. It highlights an interesting point in that some may actually be following the 'first follower' rather than you. Some people are actually so detached from the thought of being a Leader themselves that it could take quite a lot of effort for them to be convinced directly to follow a Leader. However, they will be more than willing to follow someone who is already following someone, are you following this? Do you have a 'first follower'? Is there someone in your organisation that you know if you get them on board the others will follow? If there is then go with it. Over time your leadership will influence all collectively but people develop at different rates. Leave your ego at the door and allow your 'first follower' to become a trusted member of the group. If it is working then let it work.

Without knowing it at the time I have been that 'first follower'. Sadly, in the particular role I am thinking of my boss resented the fact, rather than use the knowledge to his best advantage. He tried to belittle me in front of all of the staff and all it did was undermine his position, as everyone witnessed how he did not care for the business or me, his thoughts were only with himself. To his credit he later apologised about the whole affair and actually told me how he had resented the fact that my men, I was a Flight Commander in his Squadron, would do anything for me (not quite sure about that) and that they would only do what he wanted if I agreed, a fact rather embarrassingly backed up by my second in command during a minor disagreement with the three of us in attendance. Looking back, the sad fact for me was that he had done the hard part. He had recognised the influence I had in his Squadron but rather than include me in his decision-making process, the norm for a Flight Commander, he would undermine me. What was most disappointing for me was that I really wanted to work for him.

Can you let go sufficiently to allow your staff to be creative? Are you able to guide and influence and then step back and take stock of what is going on? You will find it a lot easier to manage multiple projects in this way. This process does not happen overnight and you will need to use your skills to develop the trust necessary to allow it to work. It does not have to be your only tactic either. Some projects are so new to a team that they may well require a more hands on approach. If that is the case then fine, do that but always be looking for the opportunity to develop your staff by giving them the opportunity to be creative.

I mentioned in the introduction about the Seven C's. I include them merely to serve as a reminder. It is important to continually assess oneself to get a handle on how we are doing, as we will not always have someone else on hand to tell us. Remember this is not an exercise in beating yourself up about something you feel you are doing wrong. We do not wish to create inner conflict. It is to simply raise awareness of where we are in the moment in order to make improvements where we may feel we would want them. Or indeed notice what is going well in order to repeat the process in the future. I include them now, towards the end of the book, because we have had a chance to cover the frame in which they are meant. We are all continually learning and whilst ensuring that you are working with The Leadership Secret will bring success, the Seven C's will give specific areas in which to focus at any one time; although that does not mean they are used in isolation, they are interwoven and underpin your behaviours. The questions I add next to the 'C's' are not exhaustive, they are to get you started. You now know enough to ask your own and conduct your own self-assessment. In addition, please include a sense of humour, it may not begin with 'C' in the English language but it will go a long way to keeping you grounded and allowing you to find a realistic perspective.

The Seven C's:
1. **Confidence** – Do I have it? Am I displaying it? What do I need to know to improve it? Am I overdoing it? Are my staff confident? What can I do in order for them to grow in confidence?
2. **Competence** – Am I taking on the right tasks? Am I being honest with myself? Is my team capable? Are we conducting the right training?
3. **Courage** – Do I have it? Am I asking the right questions before making a decision? Am I taking responsibility for my actions? Does my team have courage?
4. **Communication skills** – Are my intentions clear? Does everyone know the common goal? Am I listening? Do I allow the team to be heard? Do I speak to everyone the same or tailor to the needs of the recipient?

5. **Compassion** – Am I able to empathise? Do I know my staff? Am I assisting with their development? Am I giving myself time? Am I looking after myself?
6. **Control of my emotional state** – Am I avoiding the emotional hijack? Am I aware of my emotional state? Am I looking for ways to develop my own personal resilience?
7. **Curiosity** – Am I looking for ways to develop? What are we doing right? How can we learn?
8. **And a Sense of Humour** – Being serious does not mean you cannot have fun. Celebrate success and look for positives.

So, we are almost at the end of our journey together. In the final chapter we will look to the future for leadership as well as discuss 'The Leadership Secret'.

"Lead with the Seven C's
and
a
Sense of Humour"

Utilising Mission Trust

Points to Remember – Mission Trust:

- By explaining what is required and why, it leaves the 'how' up to a well-trained staff.

- It is important to ensure that everyone knows where their role fits in to the big picture.

- Allow latitude and empower staff to make decisions by being clear with the outcome required.

- Am I aware of the first follower?

- Am I leading with the Seven 'C's' and a sense of humour?

  - Confidence

  - Competence

  - Courage

  - Communication Skills

  - Compassion

  - Control of My Emotional State

  - Curiosity

  - And a Sense of Humour

- When the need arises, a well-led team will work for each other.

8

LOOKING TO THE FUTURE

Show that you Care about:
Those you Lead
Their development, wellbeing, sense of belonging, recognition, interests, concerns, strengths and weaknesses
The Business
Its success, development, standing and future
The Customer
Their needs, perception of you/the business
And Care about Yourself
Own development, wellbeing, and satisfaction

This is the secret to Leadership: Caring. Not over-caring, when emotions become distorted as one attempts to fully control a person, business or situation. And certainly not apathy. Apathy destroys Leadership quicker than any mistake you will ever make under good intentions. When you truly care about something/someone you give yourself the ability to make those difficult decisions because your intention will always be positive. Sometimes as Leaders it is necessary to make unpopular decisions for the good of the business or the staff and the reasons for such decisions are not always apparent to everyone. People do understand and when they trust their Leader, they will be patient. When you truly care you can become the difference that makes the difference, your passion will inspire others and you will have the courage of your conviction. You will ensure that you look after yourself as your wellbeing effects those you lead.

I was chatting with a colleague who helps to run his son's football team. Actually, he's a bit more involved than that would imply as he is the manager of one team and oversees a couple of others within the club. We were discussing this book and he stated that he was always surprised about how often the boys share their problems with him. Being a team of 15 and 16-year-olds you can imagine the range of issues that might arise. When I said it was because they see him as their Leader he seemed genuinely taken aback; "You have a common interest with them that always gives you a starting point for discussion, developing rapport. They see how committed you are to the team every game on the sideline and at training. They witness how fair you are when you make the decision to substitute your own son. You trust them to go out and perform and they trust you to help them improve. They know that you want them to win but when that doesn't happen, because no one always wins, you point them in the direction of the next game. They see how much you care. You are a Leader." What Paul does, along with many Leaders across the world, is provide a positive outlet for the youth of today. It is a cliché but today's youth must contain the Leaders of the future. What better start in life can they receive than the example of leadership?

One of the most influential Leaders, who epitomised the Leadership Secret, is the explorer Sir Ernest Shackleton; beautifully summed up in the following quote: *"For scientific discovery give me Scott; for speed and efficiency of travel give me Amundsen; but when disaster strikes and all hope is gone, get down on your knees and pray for Shackleton."* Sir Edmund Hillary. Shackleton never gave up on his team. He inspired and studied; he set example after example; he listened and made decisions, changing goals when situations changed; he cared.

Is there a leadership crisis today? Some certainly think so. There is a lot of talk about the generation of millennials growing up in an overprotected environment. Well-intentioned parents, politicians and societies went through a period of not wishing to upset anyone. School sports days were reduced to an opportunity to just take part instead of an opportunity to win something as well as lose. Someone, somewhere, thought it a good idea to remove the experience of losing. Let us imagine that they had a positive intention behind their actions and it wasn't just because they were an academic who had bad memories of sports day as a kid (although academics can be good at sport too). If it were possible to avoid losing for a whole lifetime, how boring, then there may have been a slim argument, which I would still have not agreed with. However, as we all know, life is not fair, there will be setbacks, there will be failure or feedback, depending how you look at it. Our younger years are all about learning, as are our older years but specifically when younger. This is the time to learn how to lose, and how to win for that matter. It is a time to learn about competition, strategy, preparation, about how much something means to us and how to handle emotion.

At the same time as dealing with allegedly being wrapped in cotton wool, millennials have had to deal with a new and potentially greater pressure than earlier generations ever had to. A pressure that knows no boundaries and for which there is very limited defence, social media. Social media, in the wrong hands, infiltrates even the usual safety of the home. Not only is it giving a false perception of reality but the lack of regulation also means it is a prime location for bullying. The effect of social media is still largely undetermined but it is key that we acknowledge its possibilities, positive and negative and remain attentive.

A lot of parents have asked me of the best way to assist in a child's leadership development and I have pondered this question for quite some time. Looking back over my own development as well as that of many others I have come up with a few pointers:

- Encourage children to experience as many new situations as possible. Different games, events, shops, people, cultures, activities of all kind. These do not have to be expensive; they can be a walk in the woods, travelling on a bus to an unknown town or having a conversation with an unknown adult (obviously with you present-ask a policeman for directions or something).
- Remain positive. There are enough outside agencies looking to discourage our children's development without us parents joining in. Just because you couldn't do or didn't like something that does not mean they can't or won't.
- If you want a practical course, I would advise a First Aid course at the earliest opportunity. Being a 'First Aider' teaches valuable life skills, literally. It promotes caring for oneself and others and it improves confidence. I would have it taught in all schools alongside 'Emotional State Control'.

Leadership really is for everyone. Anyone can lead by example. You may be surprised when you start doing so just how many will want to follow. If you already have that position of influence then use it wisely.

Looking to The Future

You understand how important it is to care and you can now demonstrate that 'caring' for the good of all. As we head ever closer to that incredible moment when 10 billion of us inhabit this precious planet together it is vital that effective leadership develops with the population. I will continue to champion the role Leaders play in the world as well as assisting anyone who wishes to develop. I hope that you remain curious and experiment with what you have learnt. It is only by doing that we find out who we are. My passion for leadership has grown further since taking on my most important leadership role yet, as a father to our planet's number 6,505,511,652nd human. I am sure there are many of you in a similar situation. I am sure I will continue to make mistakes but they will be from a positive intention and taken as an opportunity to learn.

In that pub garden in the Oxfordshire countryside, I knew that no small amount of luck had been involved in bringing everyone home. In a conflict zone even the best Leaders lose their soldiers, it is what happens in war and peace enforcement operations. In fact, particularly in military aviation, you don't even need to go to war for it to be risky. War is not glamorous, it is bloody and messy. It can be exhilarating, to an extent that nothing else ever quite comes close. It can also be rewarding, for no one I have ever served with can say that they haven't made a difference. Apart from the luck, throughout our time in Bosnia, I also knew that the Leadership displayed by my Troop had helped in not only bringing everyone home but in ensuring that we had done a good job. Every Private soldier had played their part; the Section Commanders had shown them an incredible example. My Troop Sergeant's unerring dedication and sense of humour along with my second in command's experience and drive. Our collective professionalism. Yes, I was a Leader by then and yes, I still had a lot to learn, which I did and improved as I did so. As I shook the hand of that truly grateful father, although I didn't know it then, he knew exactly what the secret was: "It is clear to me why you are a good Leader," he looked me straight in the eye, "because you care."

Yes, I do.

Bibliography

Branson, R. (2011). *Losing my virginity*. Random House.

Brown, D. (2007). *Tricks of the Mind*. Random House.

Cain, S. (2013). *Quiet: The power of introverts in a world that can't stop talking*. Broadway Books.

Clair, C. B. S., & Grinder, J. (2001). *Whispering in the wind*. J & C Enterprises.

Csikszentmihalyi, M. (1991). *Flow*. København: Munksgaard.

Dubrin, A. J. (2022). *Leadership: Research findings, practice, and skills*. Cengage Learning.

Gillespie, D., & Warren, M. E. (2008). *Teach yourself the Clinton factor: Communicating with charisma*. Teach Yourself.

Goleman, D. (1996). *Emotional intelligence: Why it can matter more than IQ*. Bloomsbury Publishing.

Hall, L. M., & Bodenhamer, B. G. (2002). *The User's Manual for the Brain Volume II: Mastering Systemic NLP* (Vol. 2). Crown House Publishing.

Kipling, R. (2016). *Kipling:'If–'and Other Poems*. Michael O'Mara Books.

Law, H. (2013). *The psychology of coaching, mentoring and learning*. John Wiley & Sons.

Menkes, J. (2011). *Better under pressure: How great leaders bring out the best in themselves and others*. Harvard Business Press.

Oliver, J. (2019). *The naked chef* (Vol. 1). Penguin UK.

Perkins, D. N. (2000). *Leading at the edge: Leadership lessons from the extraordinary saga of Shackleton's Antarctic expedition*. AMACOM/American Management Association.

Petrilli, L. (2011). *The Introvert's Guide to Success in Business and Leadership.* BookBaby.

Pink, D. H. (2011). *Drive: The surprising truth about what motivates us.* Penguin.

Royal Military Academy Sandhurst. Serve to Lead (an anthology). HMSO.

Salovey, P., & Mayer, J. D. (1990). Emotional intelligence. *Imagination, cognition and personality*, *9*(3), 185-211.

Seligman, M. E. (2012). *Flourish: A visionary new understanding of happiness and well-being.* Simon and Schuster.

Smith, M. (2014). *Shackleton: By endurance we conquer.* Simon and Schuster.

Thomas, M. (2011). *Loose: The Future of Business is Letting Go.* Hachette UK.

What's Next?

Should you wish to develop your organisation or yourself / your self, please contact me to arrange.

chriswhipp@me.com

www.chriswhipp.coach

Leadership Development
Organisational and Individual Resilience – Empowered Resilience
One-to-One Coaching

Printed in Great Britain
by Amazon